Radical TRUST

Manifesting a vision when it seems impossible

ANGELYN TOTH

Cover design: Jan Westendorp
Cover photo: Alex Brumm
Xenia Map Original Illustration by Karen Watson
Lynx original art by Jessie Flynn
Editor: Rebecca Hendry

ISBN 978-1775051503

Published by:

XENIACREATIONS.COM
782 Smith Road
Bowen Island, British Columbia
Canada V0N 1G2

DEDICATION

I dedicate this book to Sawyer, my grandson, who was born November 30, 2019. Thank you for showing up at this time on the planet when we need great and kind souls like you. May *Radical Trust* encourage you to follow your dreams and deliver the gifts with which you were born.

I also dedicate this book to my mother, Mary Carol Divine Rocks. I inherited my strong will from her and the courage to take on anything I dreamed of, even the impossible. She left planet earth at 54 but her spirit lives on in me and my daughter Kasara.

TABLE OF CONTENTS

FOREWORD BY JUNIE SWADRON

Dearest reader, the book you are holding in your hands will touch you in such a way that your life may never be the same again. As Angelyn herself admits, it took her twenty-five years to write it because of the vulnerability she felt every time she attempted to complete it.

Most of us know how it feels when we are guided toward something awesome but abort it lest we be judged as silly, crazy or simply outright wrong! It takes great courage to move from a life of status quo where seeming comfort allows the illusion of safety. This is a book about choosing authenticity above comfort in spite of the fear and sometimes terror.

It is this precise reason why, after reading this book, your life may never be the same. You see, Angelyn did, in fact, complete this book, and it was anything but easy. Yet she did it full out, holding nothing back. And because of her uncompromised commitment to follow her deepest knowing, the voice of her Wise Self, we do not need to take twenty years to learn what vulnerability is here to teach us. Angelyn illuminates the trail whereby not only will we never have to look back, she teaches us, through example, how we too can know the unabashed joy and freedom that comes from total surrender. Surrender to Radical Trust.

Despite the critical voices and judgments of others, even that which defied her own mind's logic, she surrendered wholly and completely. She was ready to die for a cause she had no rational understanding of. She had nothing to compare it to. Nothing in her outer world was reflecting the inner knowing she knew she had to follow no matter what.

Angelyn and I first met in 1998 on Bowen Island, a magical land off the shores of Vancouver, Canada, and we felt an immediate kinship. It was at that time that she began to write this book, and I became her writing coach. Other things took precedence in her life and in mine and then I moved away and we lost touch.

It was fifteen years before we would see each other again. We were both attending a spiritual event in Vancouver when we spotted one another. And as true friends of the heart do, we picked up where we left off as though it were only yesterday.

Within moments, Angelyn declared with excitement, "Look, Junie, I've published a book." Without hesitation, she proudly whipped out of her purse *From Squeak to Roar*, her first book, and handed it to me to admire as well. Which I did indeed!

Soon afterward she added, "Do you remember the book you were coaching me with all those years ago called *Radical Trust*?"

"Of course, I do," I replied.

Almost sheepishly, she declared, "I never finished it."

"Why is that?" I was curious to know.

"It's a difficult book to write," she explained. "It makes me feel vulnerable. It exposes so much of my inner journey. But I know it needs to be completed. Do you still do that work?" she asked.

"More than ever!" was my reply, and that began our newest sojourn, which has resulted in this splendid accomplishment.

I believe life brought us together again so I could mentor and bear witness to her almost unbelievable life journey. As well, I would learn, often through osmosis, how it feels to be utterly free. Angelyn exudes aliveness born out of years of falling down and getting up again and falling down and getting up and then staying up from all that she learned, sifted and sorted. And now, without effort, it is simply who she is. She exudes the freedom that comes when a determined woman or man crosses all barriers of traditional norms in order to heed the inner promptings of their soul and succeed.

This same passion carries over to the countless people she greets and who walk and become nourished by Xenia, an oasis of thirty-eight-acres of pristine land that she bought and developed into a retreat centre and humbly stewards.

The same holds true for the people she professionally coaches in public speaking as well as mentoring success and abundance in business. She leads from the heart of love, integrity, honour, joy and humility.

It became clear to me as we sat side by side for hours at a time to go over her manuscript that living a life of service is at the heart of her existence. Her love of truth and unfailing desire to teach others how to achieve the same inner and outer success that she has are steady companions she wakes up with every day. And you simply cannot be around Angelyn without being inspired to live your own dreams. This is what this book will do for it if you allow it. You will be stepping up to answer the call of your highest aspirations.

This book, a testament to what is possible, is Angelyn's divine heart offering to us. It's her gift of paying it forward; a book to use as a guidepost when we are floundering or searching for answers outside of ourselves. And the beauty is, we don't need a whole bunch of rituals and rules to get us there. There is only one. And that one is Radical Trust.

With deep appreciation and love,

Junie Swadron
Psychotherapist, Author and Writing Mentor
junieswadron.com

 Once you trust yourself,

you will know how to live.

—Goethe

INTRODUCTION

PART ONE is about one woman's journey through the fire of surrender into the deep pool of silence. It is a story about waking up out of the swamp of confusion the mind serves up into something far deeper that knows the truth and guides us. This book is about listening to and acting upon the messages life delivers by way of clues, symbols, relationships and encounters. Finally, *Radical Trust* can help you, the reader, find the courage to follow your own path and deliver the gifts with which you were born. It is a story of inspiration and transformation on many levels and in profound ways.

The author Angelyn says:

It took over twenty-five years to write this book. The title was clear decades earlier but the content took years to write. It was too vulnerable to share my journey because it was wrought with my own judgments and fears of what others would think. The wounds were still open, and I felt the shame, blame and embarrassment. I felt it better to wait and share the wisdom of my scars rather than my open wounds. Today it is hard to believe I travelled through many of the experiences I did.

Now I share my story because I am prompted from within and want to inspire others.

PART TWO: Angelyn shares what happens when a vision has you. You will read about a magical place: a well-known retreat centre on Bowen Island, British Columbia, Canada, and learn how it came into being and the magic of creating it with hundreds of volunteers. FINALLY, Angelyn is introduced to a powerful healing tool that would totally transform her life.

PART THREE is a journey of awakening and seeing the truth of Self.

Angelyn: *Life speaks to all of us every day and all day long. We can safely know there is a higher power guiding us. It takes courage to begin and radical trust to continue. My wish is that this book inspires you to find your own deep inner knowing by truly witnessing the feelings arising, trusting the messages being given and taking action.*

Read the metaphors and lessons and see if and how they relate to you. Become aware of the space between the lines; there you will find me.

This book may test the limits of people's perceptions and this is my intention. My job is to bring the invisible into the visible, by my seeing and sharing. Let me know how well I did.

Angelyn

Part One – The Seed of a Vision

Chapter One

MESSAGES FROM A TREEHOUSE

When the sun rose in the west
it stirred the snail
but when the rain stopped
they wrote it in the newspaper

 In the summer of 1986, I found myself living in a treehouse on an enchanted Island off the west coast of Canada. **Bowen Island** has a traditional **name** in the Squamish language, Nexwlelexwm meaning "Fast Drumming Ground.

Precipitated by my best friend's (what she called) soul assignment, I jumped unabashadly into the abyss.

When Chrystalle entered my life, she shook up my reality and played havoc with my programming. Her first job was to help me to S T O P. She jokingly said it was one of her toughest assignments.

I kept busy in the corporate world, commuting in from the suburbs every day. In spite of feeling burned out, I kept going like the Energizer Bunny. Many times on my commute, I heard myself pleading inwardly, "Stop the world; I want to get off!" I was such a comtemplative person, needing nature and alone time to recharge my batteries, but at this particular stage, there was no time for that, nor was there even the awareness it was missing. My life had become so harried, mostly from distractions in an attempt to block the pain of a failing marriage and much self-doubt.

I told my husband I needed to go away to write a book for my business, and taking a couple of months away of uninterrupted time would be the most efficient plan.

My husband was alarmed at the idea of me taking a sabbatical and thought I had lost my mind. My dad phoned me from England, asking what I was doing going to a treehouse. And to do what?? And why couldn't I just be normal, settle down and have a baby or something? When I shared that I wanted to write a book for my business, he commented, "What do you have to write that anyone would want to read?" He was negative about the whole idea. Bless him, he didn't even know he was.

So much resistance came from the outside world, but this irresistible urge led me out of my crazy-making life in downtown Vancouver and placed me, gently, into a rich and fulfilling plane destined to honour my calling.

I began my adventure on Bowen Island with a contract I had to lead a weekend workshop for twenty corporate managers at the CNIB (Canadian National Institute for the Blind) Retreat Centre. And to make it extra special, my friend Sandy sailed me over to the island in his beautiful yacht the day before the program started. I'll never forget because when we anchored close to our destination and looked up to the sky, a rainbow bridge glowed from Horseshoe Bay to Bowen Island. If Sandy hadn't seen it as well, I would have thought it an hallucination. I've never seen a rainbow spanning a clear blue summer sky before, but there it shone: some kind of augury, and a magical sign for sure.

The moment I stepped foot on Bowen Island, it was love at first sight—my soul recognized home in a way I'd only ever felt in special places that usually involved an expanse of land, trees, birds and stillness.

I couldn't wait to complete my program so I could get on with my time alone.

The workshop was successful and provocative, and I did put my heart and soul into it. By Sunday evening, I was ready to visit the place that would become my sanctuary for the next two-and-a-half months.

Arriving at the treehouse, I was captivated by how charming and quaint it was, nestled high up in the trees. It had a small kitchen area, an upstairs loft, fireplace, and even a shower with hot water. There were windows everywhere including the roof and the walls, like a green house and quite exposed to the road below but I never felt concerned about my privacy. Though tiny in size, it felt big in space and pure in essence. The living area was neutral, not cluttered with other people's energies or things. It would become my incubator, my fort, and my salvation. In order to honour my plan to stay isolated and quiet, I didn't have a phone and left my car with Chrystalle so she could run my office in my absence. I kept to myself completely, not socialising and not connecting with any humans.

Other than Chrystalle's occasional visits, I stayed alone. And it didn't feel easy. I was afraid of the dark, so I kept a little light on most of the time and didn't go out at night. Being alone became an extraordinary experience and a transformative time in my life.

The first week passed in pure and utter bliss, which surprised me. I suspected I was being given some grace before the real work kicked in—a bit like the romantic stage of a relationship or the calm before the storm.

I didn't have the funds to take this sabbatical, but I planned to live a minimalist style while there. After paying the rent, I had little money left over for food, so I bought inexpensive items like potatoes and carrots. I share this because, even though I had little money in my pocket, I felt rich, blessed and abundantly wealthy to be living in this magical treehouse on Bowen Island for the whole summer.

Two weeks later Chrystalle met me down at Snug Cove, the little village where the ferry came in, about half an hour's walk from the treehouse. She did a double take when she saw me skipping across the road to greet her. My usual makeup, primped hair, high heels and business suit were missing—instead, awe and gratitude shone from my shiny bare face. I wore plain clothes and sneakers. She said I looked like a teenager and felt curious as to what happened. Simplicity had captured my heart, and I had come home. It was the most wondrous, peaceful journey inward.

Mother Nature became my friend, and a place in my soul I had lost touch with opened up again. Being alone in the woods brought bliss into my very being, and I knew I could never go back to the busy world from which I had come.

I had fallen in love. In love with this new freedom and simplicity. I had embarked on an adventure and opened to what was shown to me.

Shortly after this, the tide turned, and for the next month I found it hard to stay alone. Negative and attacking self-talk replaced the bliss and ecstasy. My ego mind wanted me away from this situation immediately because it lost ground each day I stayed there. On a few occasions, I caught myself bolting for the ferry in an attempt to escape but resisted just before boarding. Instead, I dragged myself back to the treehouse and hung on for dear life.

I remember the pain revealed through the silence. It took every bit of restraint I had to cope with the layers of internalised oppression. I understood why people shied away from silence. It was too intimate and too threatening to parts of myself that didn't want to know the truth of how I felt.

This was not what I had bargained for or signed up for, but apparently, it was. Many days and weeks passed in this distress.

Until one day the clouds lifted, and I realized I would be okay. I even had glimpses of extreme pleasure, which I found in nature in the most primal of ways.

Walking the trails beside Killarney Lake I felt a deepening of connection inwards to unnamed and unknown parts of myself. One day, wandering up an overgrown pathway, it became obvious from the autumn leaves fallen from the previous year that not too many people came this way. A river ran just below, with lots of decaying branches and stones creating a mini dam across its path. I climbed under the fallen trees and stepped my way across the river using the stones and logs as a bridge. On the other side, Mother Nature had so graciously left a log, serving as a bench for me to sit on. I perched beside lush, full-grown ferns and marvelled at the complexity of Mother Nature's plan.

Observing a spider's web, I considered the ingenious nature of this creature. Casting a web to catch its food, just like a fisherman putting out his net. Spiders had become quite a part of my life since living at the treehouse, and it was hard to believe how terrified of them I used to be. One particular spider became part of my family as I watched it behind my bed building its web, and I couldn't help but study its patience and prowess. I was fascinated by the spider's incredible magnetic charm, drawing its survival to itself. They do not usually move once they have cast their web. They sit and wait in a gentle yin expectancy.

The sound of the river shifted my attention back, its motion purposeful and consistent. An inner whisper tempted me to go into the river to taste its water and experience its energy. At first I hesitated until I felt a sense of gentle encouragement.

I climbed down by the river and felt the pulse as it flowed around my legs, undaunted by my presence. Crouching, I sat atop one of the large stones in the river.

Four hours slipped by as I became one with all that was. There was no separation.

My reverie was finally broken when I caught a glimpse of two ears behind one of the tall ferns. Quietly, I lifted myself up and eased over toward them, keeping my head low and my movements slow. Suddenly, right in front of me, a deer popped its head up and looked me straight in the eyes. We both startled, but luckily it didn't run away; instead, it carried on grazing, keeping a close eye on me.

I basked in the beauty and abundance of nature, watching the butterflies and various birds. Gratefully, I took in the fragrances offered, feeling like my heart was bursting open. I remembered my oneness and connectedness to all that is. To God and all life. It had been so long and so many years since I had managed to experience nature this way, and I vowed never to separate from this again.

It was here in this moment that the seed of a vision got planted in my psyche. I didn't know fully what it was, but it had to do with the essence of silence, nature and holding a space for people to experience its profound gifts. In my mind's eye I saw a beautiful retreat centre with animals and fields, trees, creeks, gardens and swings. I felt deeply this would be part of my destiny even though I had no idea how I would afford such a dream.

This became a hugely significant reference point for me to use, many years later, in my work with others.

Back at the treehouse, I made peace with my commitment to staying there and doing the work I planned for my business. I started writing, and the most unexpected information came to me. An interesting process unfolded; a kind of relationship with my computer began and took on a life of its own. I would throw random questions on the computer screen and experience profound answers responding from the deepest part of myself—answers I had no previous knowledge of, and at first, it startled me. Where did this information come from, and what was going on? This became the direction and focus of my time, and I left my original plan of a business book behind.

That wasn't the only unusual thing that happened while I lived in the treehouse; there were other mystical and other-worldly things as well. One night, I was typing away in the wee hours of the morning, which became a writing rhythm I adopted naturally, when suddenly, the cup and saucer by my computer moved across the desk at least eight to ten inches. I freaked out, what on earth just happened?

I thought something terrible and frightening might follow, like perhaps an alien visitation or ghost. It scared the living daylights out of me. Terrified, I slowly shut down the computer and slithered up the ladder to the loft, keeping my back tight to the wall and leaving all the lights on. I lay in bed sweating, begging, "I'm not ready, I'm not ready."

After an hour or so, sleep overcame me. I stayed deep in thought the whole next day. Wondering about worlds beyond my present construct of reality. When I'd agreed to do this retreat, I'd had no idea what the greater plan for me might entail. It felt guided from the beginning of this ordeal, including how easily the treehouse became available to me. In spite of the scary experiences I was having, my implicit faith, coupled with my determination, kept me on the island.

Over the following several evenings, I experienced many teachings about cellular transformation and dematerialization. I was shown how apparent solid forms, like a wall, are not solid at all but a wave frequency. Instead, particles actually have space between them and the ability to morph and pass through each other. I was shown energy frequencies, colours and other dimensions I had not been aware of before. Just for the record, I did not have any hallucinogenic substances with me: only the prolonged time spent alone in nature with no distractions.

During my sojourn in the treehouse, I felt the presence of a baby awaiting my attention. I sensed it wanted me to agree to become its mother. How absurd; I didn't particularly want children. It had never been my thing, so why would I say yes, especially in a rocky marriage? It became persistent, and it was annoying since my marriage was probably over anyway. Nevertheless, I felt a whispering spirit asking me to become its mother. Tormented by this proposition, I found myself observing the lady next door playing in the back yard with her young children. I had to contort my body over the deck to be able to watch and not be noticed because I didn't want to draw attention to myself. I thought being a mother was not my path. I had barely held a child before and had little interest. Nevertheless, I found myself obsessing over this request. It felt ridiculous and out of context with my life.

A strange thing occurred next. I got the message that this being would come in "for" five years. Not "in" five years: the message was clearly "for" five years. I didn't understand what this meant and dismissed it from my mind.

Several days later, the nudging from this being started again, and more out of frustration than real willingness, I finally agreed. "Okay, for Pete's sake, yes, but for now, leave me alone."

Soon, a feeling of deep inner peace enveloped me, and I thought, *oh good this spirit has given up*. But how wrong I got it. I did, after all, say yes.

When I moved into the treehouse, it was under the premise of writing a book for my business, focussing on communications and personal development. Instead, I wrote two manuscripts, *Messages from a Tree House* and *The Story of Cabroi* (see tape version). This was totally different than what I had imagined writing. The manuscript foretold the consciousness shift over the next two decades and new paradigms opening in myself and in the world.

I learned so much about myself during this incubation, but the thing I was most grateful for was being transported back to myself, to my soul, and to nature. It formed part of a divine plan that is still unfolding, and from hindsight, it was an initiation and preparation for something far greater yet.

The last few days of my pilgrimage became full of surprises. While staying at the treehouse, I had kept to myself. I didn't accept rides to and from Snug Cove, and I didn't have visitors or a phone line (this was before everyone owned a cell phone). I was not socializing at all. I marvelled at how successful I was with this intention. In fact, I didn't see one other person on any of my hikes in the woods during the whole time there, and it had been a beautiful summer. It was the year Vancouver hosted Expo 86, and I think everybody went there rather than visiting Bowen.

During the last few days I was wondering who my neighbours were as I prepared for the outside world again. Two days before I left, I had a woman, presumably a neighbour, come right up the back stairs of the treehouse and catch me off-guard, saying, "Hi, I'm from across the way and wanted to invite you to a neighbourhood barbecue we're having on the beach tomorrow."

I agreed to go and thought, *what perfect timing*. Chrystalle would have come over by then, and we could go together. The other wish I had was to ride a horse through the trails, and this would offer the ultimate completion to my fantasy experience on Bowen.

At the barbecue the next day I thoroughly enjoyed meeting new friends and hearing stories of their lives on Bowen. They shared their curiosity about what I was working on since they could clearly see me up there in the treehouse typing over the months. The amazing bonus came from a woman at the barbecue who offered me her horse to ride through the trails. She said, "Yes, you can ride him anytime. When would you like to?" I looked her straight in the eye and said with such confidence and eagerness, "How about right now?" She agreed, and before anyone could blink, I was saddled up and riding Calla down the road.

Chrystalle had never seen me on or around horses before and said she was shocked by my prowess as she watched me tacking up and handling the horse. It came as instinctual and familiar to me, and my cells shivered with delight because horses were my first real passion. My dad always told the story of how I left home at age six and took to the woods with my pretend horse, jam sandwiches and vast imagination. Soon my imagination manifested into reality, and I spent most of my childhood and teen years cleaning stables in exchange for riding lessons. I later left England to teach riding in Upstate New York in one of the Camp America programs. Horses filled me with love, and I always felt at home in their presence.

Entering the park trail to the lake, I began cantering

along this lovely wide pathway through the woods. I had a huge smile on my face, and I was feeling like the luckiest person alive. Oh, what bliss and joy. The Angels had come, and boy, did I ever feel grateful. It was the most wonderful completion to my journey on Bowen Island, and what a manifestation. How my life had changed since entering this magical island.

When my husband came to pick me up on the last day, we had an unfamiliar ease with each other. We seemed close and playful for the first time in years. To my great surprise, we made love. It was spontaneous and unexpected. And then it happened: the moment I "knew" we had conceived the resolute spirit who had bugged me for weeks. Oh, my God, what had I done. In spite of our differences, we had conceived this child in love. The only way she would have wanted it.

To leave the treehouse and Bowen Island was hard for me. My heart and soul ached to remain on this incredible island. Certainly, I did achieve my goal of "stopping." It became the most wondrous, peaceful journey inward. Mother Nature became my friend again like in my childhood, and a place in my soul I had lost touch with over the years had opened wide once more. I had grown so at peace at the treehouse and knew I had been changed forever by this experience. I made a promise to myself that day to return and buy a house on Bowen Island. Little did I know this aligned my path and prepared me for a future I couldn't even imagine.

Ten Years Earlier:

Chapter Two

THE NIGHT I PRAYED

Deception is a funny thing
bent on destruction
but offering the child a flower
Sweet daisy smashed like pulp
into the wet earth
She is left astonished

I was a late bloomer when it came to intimate relationship. Lacking experience and confidence in myself, I was naïve and vulnerable. So, it was no surprise when I fell for a much older man with persuasive charms. I was twenty-two at the time, and he was forty-one; quite an age gap.

He was a wild and crazy, artistic Italian with a larger-than-life personality. He treated me like his princess for the first year and I bought the fairy-tale story lock, stock and barrel. I was captivated by him from the first moment

21

I saw him trip over the curb at an event put on by the radio station I worked for. Later I found out it was a setup to get my attention. He was a very successful designer who didn't like the spotlight but was always making people laugh or surprising them. He mesmerized me with his pranks, and we had so much fun together.

Given how much older he was, I knew he had been married before and had children, but I didn't know the truth about him for the longest time. I believed he was divorced but found out way later (when it was too late from my heart's point of view) he was still married with five kids. He would go back and forth from his home to mine, and he did whatever he wanted, like staying out all night (with me). Once I found out, I hated that I was having an affair with a married man, but it seemed hard to let go of him, and he wouldn't let me. When I tried to walk away, he got very domineering and I started to feel a subtle fear arising.

I remember a song that came out at that time, released by Rod Stewart, called "If loving you is wrong, I don't wanna be right." This was my story, and though wrong, I couldn't help myself. His jealousy became prevalent, along with his controlling behaviour. After the first year, things changed, and instead of being enamoured with his tactics and displays of love, I became afraid. He owned me. Unfortunately, the fairy tale didn't end happily ever after; instead, it ended in court.

After an explosion of anger, he would say, "But I love you," and this was supposed to make it right again. And for a while it did, but it was a counterfeit for love and an addictive drug.

I remember walking barefoot over the old Cambie Street Bridge in the middle of the night, having just escaped the wrath of this man's temper. Another time he chased me up a one-way road in his car, going the wrong way. One time a romantic "bicycle-built-for-two" ride in Stanley Park ended up with a violent slap across the face and vicious accusations made about me apparently looking at some other man. There was blood on my face, and a group of men saw what happened and started walking over to protect me. He shouted fiercely at them that it was none of their business, and to my absolute surprise they backed off.

In restaurants I had to monitor where my eyes were because he was constantly accusing me of looking at other men, even though I had zero interest in anyone else. The jealousy was intense, and after a while, my life-force was choked behind an "eyes-down-don't-breathe-or-you'll-get-killed" existence.

One day after a violent argument I said I was done and going to leave the relationship. We were stopped at the side of the road and before I could get out of the car, he took off locking the car door. He drove out to Spanish Banks Beach all the while threatening me and begging me not to leave. It was late and dark as he pulled into the parking lot. I was afraid because there was nobody around. He jumped out of the car and ran out to the ocean and started walking in saying he was going to kill himself. I knew he couldn't swim so I went running in after him. I tried pulling him out but he shoved me away and kept walking in deeper and deeper.

I panicked and begged him to stop but he kept plunging himself into the water and choking. Finally I screamed: "OK, ok I will not leave – just get out". Soon he turned around and came out and we drove home in silence with our wet clothes soaking the car seats. This was the beginning of the end, but the unspoken contract of abuse was not yet finished.

I hated the nights he came home after midnight with a hamburger for me and insisted I wake up and eat it. Practically gagging on every mouthful, I swallowed back the war. Eventually, I started fighting back and couldn't believe my anger and strength.

My sister came over to Canada for nearly a year and witnessed much of what happened in this relationship but not all of it. She said it was volatile and I was just as eruptive as he was. One night I had to drive him to

Emergency after piercing his skull with my keys. This energy called "love" brought out the worst in both of us.

The pain of what I thought was love felt excruciating. He was so much older, and I felt powerless to walk away because I perceived him as having control over my life and, truth be known, there also existed the side that lured me—his spontaneous nature and undying, obsessive love for me. Who wouldn't want to be loved that much? At least, that's what I thought it was. His tenacious passion and attention fixed on me kept me there. It was a drug to which I became addicted. Yes, I loved the attention, but soon the imprisonment of this had its price to pay.

One time he was in my apartment looking for something to eat and started raging because there was nothing available in my fridge. Granted, the fridge and cupboards were pretty bare because we ate out most of the time. One day after work, I walked into my kitchen and saw evidence my boyfriend had stopped by. He had made me give him a key to my apartment. There was a loaf of bread on the counter, which was definitely not there when I left for work. I opened the cupboard to put the bread away and discovered my cupboards were stuffed to the gills with food; tins, packets, containers— Oh my God, what has he been up to? I threw open the fridge door and the fridge was full of fresh produce, fruit, milk, cheese, cold cuts and so much more. It was enough food to feed a family of four for a month. I pulled out a bag that was squeezed into the centre of the fridge. It clearly wasn't food. Ripping it open like a kid at Christmas, I found a pair of high-priced jeans. *Wow, he is nuts*, I thought. It became a bitter, sweet dilemma.

Eventually, the roller-coaster ride of love and war proved too much to bear, and one day I packed up and left the country. I knew he wouldn't follow me because he had a phobia of flying. What I didn't bargain on was how he would follow me emotionally. Denny Boyd, a columnist for the *Vancouver Sun,* wrote three articles about a trans-oceanic love story prompted by this desperate man. When I got to England, I couldn't believe my eyes when I saw my name strewn across billboards;

See Chapter 7 regarding my name change

there were three in different parts of my hometown. One outside the bus station, one outside the post office and one in the middle of the town square. My name was across the top, and the message read, *I love you and always will,* followed by his name.

It must have cost him a fortune, and people thought he was crazy but romantic. Several local news reporters knocked at the door asking for an interview about the billboards, but we never told them anything. It was embarrassing.

My family didn't know the extent of the physical and emotional abuse I had endured with him. In fact, nobody knew—I had kept it a secret.

After a few weeks, his telephone calls and pleas for forgiveness got the better of me and, unbelievable as it may seem, I left England and returned to Vancouver.

Needless to say, it didn't take long before the abuse started again, and I felt trapped and full of despair. I loved this man intensely with all my heart, and the idea of leaving him felt impossible. But the emotional abuse was a never-ending torture, and I internalized the belief I was worthless, and it had all been my fault. His aggression escalated and the final straw came shortly thereafter.

I knew my life was at risk if I stayed with this man any longer, and I decided to pack up my things and get the hell out of there. I started packing frantically to leave, not expecting him back for at least a couple of hours. Then to my horror I saw him from the bedroom window, crossing the road toward the townhouse. *Oh, my God.* I panicked. This would not be pretty. I braced myself for impact as he came through the door, and when he caught wind of what I was up to, he grabbed my suitcase and clothes and threw them across the room, shouting, "You're not going anywhere!"

The next few hours were terrifying, as he yelled and ripped out the telephone wires and chained the doors. He made it perfectly clear I had become his prisoner. In my haste to escape, I made a run for the large window and was about to crash through it with my shoulder when he grabbed me. I screamed, but since the neighbours had grown used to such noises coming from my place, it was futile. He flung me on the couch and held a pillow over my face for what seemed like an eternity. The more I struggled, the harder he pushed the pillow into my face, and I thought I would surely suffocate.

From a place deep within, I heard myself praying into the void, "Dear God, I don't know what to do. Please, help me." It was the first time I had prayed in years, and it came from such a deep inner space. I started to feel a calm silence enter my very being. I now know it was the beginning of radical trust for me, where I knew with certainty I was protected. Even if it meant my death.

Finally, he released the pillow and let me go.

I sat comatose on the couch for ages and was surprised to find myself still alive hours later. The next thing I remembered was him coming over with a bucket of warm water, saying, "Sorry, sweetheart. I'll get help tomorrow, I promise." This was a promise he had made many times, but he never followed through. He told me he loved me and proceeded to wash my feet in this bucket, pleading for me to forgive him. I no longer understood the word "love"; surely this wasn't it.

He went to bed, and I stayed awake in the living room, clutching a pillow all night. I sensed if I tried to escape, he would actually kill me. My chances seemed better to stay quiet until the morning. I didn't sleep a wink.

In the middle of the night, physically and emotionally drained, I went into the bathroom. Catching a glimpse of myself in the mirror, I walked over to the sink and looked deep into my own eyes with a feeling of complete surrender. It was as if I had handed my life over and had no more fear. Emptiness engulfed me, and my mind stopped. It was over. I had gone back numerous times before, but this time was different. Something had shifted. The contract was done. Dead or alive, it mattered not. I knew it was the truth and I knew this I could trust.

The next morning, he dropped me off at work, saying he loved me and was sorry and would pick me up at lunch time as usual. I remained quiet and walked away from the car and away from this man forever.

In my office, a colleague asked what had happened to me. I said nothing had. She asked me to go into the bathroom with her and, as I walked in, I saw the giveaway signs in the mirror. My face and neck were full of fiery red blotches. She said, "What did he do this time?"

Reluctantly, I told her, and she phoned the police and reported him, despite my begging her not to. "He will kill me," I pleaded. She assured me she would protect me.

They detained him for all of an hour and a half before releasing him; he had used a connection with a corrupt police chief.

However, he didn't get away with it in court. He was found guilty of "a cowardly crime," as the judge put it that day.

At first, I had to go into hiding from his obsessive pursuits, which lasted years in spite of his arrest and restraining order.

He followed me around for the next three years, secretly and sometimes not so secretly. I would see his car drive slowly by my house. It creeped me out how obsessed he was, and one day, the stalking ended.

As far as relationships went after that, I felt a little gun shy, to put it mildly. I stayed away from dating and places where I might meet guys. Instead I pursued my healing journey and simply made my way in the world. Nightmares though, followed me around for decades.

Chapter Three

COURAGE TO GROW

Courage
like the quiet drops of rain
needs little fanfare
But an ocean of
Remembrance

 In 1981, I got a job at the Royal Bank head office in downtown Vancouver, and there, on the 35th floor, I met my husband. He worked in Agricultural Financing and I worked in Marketing. This gorgeous man had invited me out for a drink a number of times, but I kept refusing, not trusting how such a stunning and charismatic six-foot-four guy would have any interest in little ole me. Aside from the fact I couldn't trust anyone after my previous ordeal, I noticed the women in the office swooned around him. He seemed a bit of a lady's man, and I remained cautious.

One day, this attractive man came into my office cubicle and started up a conversation about horses and how much he loved them. Scepticism was my first reaction, given I had my desk and walls covered with horse pictures. He invited me to ride his horse, and I thought that was the worst pick-up line I had ever heard.

"No, no," he tried to assure me, looking at the horse pictures. "I do really have a horse. His name is Justice, and he's a thoroughbred."

Eventually, this tenacious man convinced me to go out to his parents' forty-acre farm in the Fraser Valley, where I did indeed meet Justice.

When I arrived I could see him and his father busy working out by the barn. As I approached, I saw they were assisting the local vet, steering young bullocks into a contraption to restrain them while they got castrated. Ouch.

My suitor wore jeans and a western shirt, and he had ruffled hair and a big smile on his face as he greeted me. The business suit and playboy persona had gone, and instead a genuine, almost shy man stood before me. From that point forth, I got well and truly hooked and felt so blessed this wonderful guy felt interested in me and had a horse to boot. Wow, how lucky can one girl get?

Little did he know at the time that he had picked me up out of the gutter of despair and dusted me off and given me a safe place to land.

I was so scarred by the previous relationship that it took a fair bit of gentle coaxing to trust again. However, I became rather attracted to this man with the horse. We started dating, and I could feel we had a certain kind of destiny together. It was not wild chemistry so much as it felt like "by divine appointment." Within a couple of years, we got married in all the traditional rituals one would expect from a Hungarian Catholic boy and an English Catholic girl, even though neither of us practiced this religion. And because my mother had fallen sick and was unable to travel to Canada, we went and got married again in England the following week before taking our honeymoon in Paris. It was literally the full deal all over again, but with all my friends and family in England. I wore my same white wedding dress, and he wore his tux. We got chauffeured to an old English church in a white Rolls Royce, read our vows to each other one more time, and had our marriage blessed. Wow, that should have sealed the deal forever.

Our honeymoon in Paris was a precious time for us to be together in Europe exploring a different culture. I loved this man so much, and we had a sweet time.

Back home, I remember commuting to work feeling like the luckiest girl alive who was married to this gorgeous and smart man.

My conditioning encouraged me to take on all the household chores like cooking and cleaning, and my husband was the man whose work was the most important thing. Very quickly we had established a traditional marriage. I attended formal events as the wife of an important Royal Bank farming executive. They were full of shop talk and I understood very little of the conversations, nor did I have anything in common with the other wives. I was feeling a bit awkward, bored and like a square peg in a round hole.

I never felt very important being a woman, and any effort I took towards furthering my career was met with a pat on the head and a *there, there,* meaning "you don't have to do anything other than a regular job."

Within the first year my wife role felt empty and uninspiring. I knew there was something in me needing to express and expand. We lived on a small, four-acre broiler farm with a quota of 50,000 chickens. My husband was a good farmer and made sure everything was as clean as possible, and he culled the injured birds every day. I hated witnessing the nights at the end of the cycle when the chicken catchers arrived and took the chickens into the crates and drove them to their demise. My husband would have loved me to work in his office at the processing plant, which he also owned, but I couldn't be part of killing chickens all day long. I was empty inside because I had no connection to nature, and my soul suffered. A big gaping hole lay inside, and I thought my husband and domestic life should fill it. But it didn't.

My journey of awakening had started that awful night of terror where I nearly ended up murdered. It was the first time I had prayed with sincerity, even though I was raised in the church and praying was what we did.

This, as I recall, is when a fork in the road appeared and I was to choose between numbing my reality or exploring further horizons. A dissatisfaction with life had taken hold and an insatiable seeking had begun. I didn't even know what I was seeking but it was intrinsic and a yearning to understand my true nature.

My religion took a turn into a spiritual quest, and it was a solo journey. My husband couldn't relate; he was a scientist and I was a mystic. Sometimes on my bus commute I would find myself sitting next to a person and a spiritual conversation ensued. Finding the odd companion in the world felt reassuring.

With my husband, and previously with my dad, I used to hide my books and a big chunk of who I was for fear of ridicule. This, I admit, mostly came down to my insecurity, and it was many years before "self-actualization" became more mainstream. I couldn't show up fully as myself in the relationship but only as this person I thought I *should be.*

This same dilemma flowed over into my work.

My nine-to-five job at the Royal Bank had become a prison sentence to my soul. Working on the 35th floor of a big tower was too far from the ground, and especially from nature.

I continued for several years even though deep down I was curious as to my true calling. I had no real idea what this was, yet there was a yearning down in my soul nudging me forward.

One day, as fate would have it, a brochure about a public speaking workshop came across my desk. Like many people, this was my greatest fear. I would get red with embarrassment when speaking at a meeting with more than a couple of people present. This impeded my growth and ability to share my ideas, so the course called to me. I asked my boss if the company would pay for me to do the workshop because it would improve my ability to speak at meetings and, sure enough, they approved my request.

When people say a particular workshop changed their life, I have to agree. Attending this program changed my life profoundly. By the end of the weekend, I could stand up and speak without a red face and terror surging through my body. I learned how to think on my feet and become present to the audience. It felt surprising and transformational.

At the end, I asked the instructor, Harold, what it would take to lead this program. I was astounded by how this question came out of me. I thought he would say it would take having a psychology degree. I had observed how and when Harold moved people from chair to chair and group to group, and his precision struck me. *There must be more going on than meets the eye,* I thought. The results seemed astounding, and it had to be the process that moved things along, though you had to know how to wield the tool. The instructor looked at me intently and replied, "Well, you would make a great facilitator. If you want, I will teach you."

You should have seen the shock on my face when Harold made this offer.

When I met him in his late seventies, he had barely taught anyone how to lead his program, which seemed surprising given how brilliant it was. So, mentor me he did, for three long and arduous years. I say that because he was a difficult person to please when he wasn't in front of the room. He was a perfectionist on the one hand and so disorganized on the other. Still, he loved his program. It was his baby. It was life changing, and I had a hunger to learn.

One day, I went to my boss at the Royal Bank and asked if I could go part-time. He said no right-away because it wasn't customary back then in the corporate offices. Never being good at taking no for an answer, I wrote a five-page letter outlining how it could work by farming certain projects out to different departments and said they could even save money. My proposition, surprisingly, got accepted, and for the next two years, I worked part time with the Royal Bank and the rest of the time with Harold.

By the time Harold passed away, I led eighty percent of the program. I travelled with him to Toronto and worked with big corporations like IBM, Bank of Montreal, Vancouver Board of Trade and many others. He proved gracious at letting me fall flat on my face, picking me up, and making it right for me numerous times. Never did he try to embarrass me, so he handed me small cards with instructive messages on them as we moved around the workshop room. I remain forever grateful to Harold for his unwavering belief in me and for giving me the opportunity to turn my life around.

Chapter Four

ADDICTION AND SURRENDER

Trust fall
everything
all
the death and
the birth

As my modest career took off, I started my own business, *Leading Edge Creative Development Ltd.* This included facilitating stress-management programs and public-speaking workshops, and I was surprised myself with how much I loved it.

At the same time, an even bigger gap arose between me and my husband. I wish I could have reported that we lived happily ever after, like I had always imagined. Fundamentally, our perspectives were completely different, and through a lack of a common language to understand each other's world, our marriage became the loneliest and some of the most difficult years of my life. I didn't understand how compatibility played an important role in marriage. We had very little in common, we had different spiritual beliefs and values and we were strangers to each other in many ways. Any move toward intimacy felt difficult and scary; a chasm developed between us.

As we distanced from each other, the house became empty and lonely. Profound despair developed at the pit of our relationship because we did not communicate the truth to each other or ourselves. It became evident the separateness happened because of the dark secret we withheld from one another. Both addicts, neither one knew the nightmare the other lived. Secretly, silently, we were both killing ourselves.

I had developed an eating disorder from the middle-of-the-night force-feeding I had endured from the previous destructive relationship. Long after that relationship ended, the wounds were still sore and the habit continued. I would eat then throw up in the bathroom. But more than a habit, it became an addiction. I didn't understand what had happened to me except that I felt ashamed. It turned into the most self-destructive experience of my life.

My husband spent his days and evenings working. Either he worked away from home, out in the barn or at his desk. But he was always working. We became two strangers in the same household. His workaholism led him to the discovery of drugs to prop him up and keep him going. Unfortunately, it escalated into a serious addiction that took a hold on his life.

Within me, a deep split had occurred. I never felt good enough. This manifested as an obsession with my weight and trying to get thinner, even though my weight was normal. I felt desperately lonely and longed to regain who I used to be before this addiction took over my life. My days were spent working, eating, running ten kilometres or attending intensive fitness programs, one after another. I had fallen into an addictive pattern and implored every day for it to stop. At lunchtimes, I went to the men's YMCA and ran track with them in the gym, round and round, for nearly an hour every workday, hiding this ferocious monster that lurked close by. I also joined the women's YWCA and took fitness courses I qualified to teach but never did. I just kept running and running. Running away from what? I did not know.

The purging habit had taken control of my life. I would stuff my stomach to breaking point, then throw up, and on an empty stomach, would run at least ten kilometres to punish myself. At the time, I didn't realise I was running away from the pain of a larger hurt deep in my psyche going back to my earliest years as a child, when my mother who had a drinking problem told me about the abuse in her life over and over and over again. Every week, my dad went out to the pub, and my sister was old enough to go out with friends. I was the only one left at home and therefore the target to sit and listen to my mother as she sipped wine and drank back her pain. In the end, I could almost recite every word of her stories of being raped at sixteen and of all the anguish she endured under the rule of an evil stepmother. I dreaded hearing them one more time, even though I felt sorry for her. It was a lot for a twelve-year-old to take on.

Decades later, living in another country, I'm dealing with my own stories of pain and addiction. I remember the days driving through Vancouver and heading into the doughnut shop to purchase my fix and taking in a moment of satisfaction before crashing back into the pit of despair. Next, I'd go in search of a clean-enough washroom to vomit up the emotional pain once again. Every day, I told myself I wouldn't do it that day; after all, I was a strong and intelligent person. I questioned why I couldn't stop. What did I have wrong with me? But it was in vain, as the insidious creature had taken a hold on my life in spite of my strong will and intentions.

The feeling of separation and fear carved deep grooves into my heart. I could barely look into my eyes in the mirror because it reflected such self-hatred. The very presence of the sun posed a threat to my darkness. This nightmare went on for four harrowing years.

In spite of all this, I continued working and leading stress-management workshops for adults. Showing up with my business suit and high-heeled shoes, I became masterful at hiding the truth. Can you imagine the contradiction in this? Eventually, my integrity, or lack thereof, stared me in the face and I knew I had to stop and get help.

Back then, too little had been written about these eating disorders known as bulimia and anorexia, and so I felt completely alone and desperate. In fact, I'd never even heard of it, yet it consumed my days and nights. What I would eat and how I would get rid of it stayed front and centre in my mind. It seemed as if an evil force lived inside me that couldn't be satisfied. During those years, I didn't have a friend I felt safe enough to confide in, so the torture and loneliness became crippling.

Upon seeking whatever plan could work, I thought the most difficult thing I could do was to tell my husband and then the problem would stop for sure. I told him, and he listened with such sweet warmth and caring, it quite surprised me. Then he said, "Don't worry. You just need to get some help. It's probably because you have some deeper unresolved issues."

Wow, I appreciated his genuine kindness. Unfortunately, it didn't stop the disorder from happening; I just felt more vulnerable and self-conscious because he now knew what I got up to.

Next, I tried seeking help through the traditional psychologist route but felt further shamed by their approach. They said stupid things like, "Just stop doing it." Can you imagine telling an alcoholic or drug addict to just stop doing it? "Of course, I would if I could, you idiot!" screamed my wounded self. One doctor said, "Throw up in a jar, and this will be enough to disgust you from doing it ever again." Little did he know about this illness and little did he care.

One day, while listening to a talk show on a local radio station, I heard a man by the name of Jim Tolchard speaking about healing eating disorders with the help of a process called NLP (Neuro-Linguistic Programming) along with Core Belief Reprogramming. My ears perked up, and I listened intently to what he said. It interested me because I had never listened to talk radio at home before. It became one of those subtle guidance messages I would one day wake up to fully.

The next day, I booked an appointment under the guise of getting the information for my clients. I couldn't possibly admit I had a problem. The shame and humiliation about this behaviour loomed enormous. On my way there, I rehearsed my story. I arrived on time, donned with my business suit and mask.

My first encounter with Jim and his partner Elly Roselle was exposing but they both had such a disarming approach. Jim asked me questions and Elly held the space and took notes. They were both perfect listeners. Against my original intention, I found myself pouring out my heart and soul, including telling them of this purging habit. My face heated up with embarrassment, and this breach of trust at the promise I had made to myself shocked me. Without judgment, they worked with me for over three hours, which seemed like minutes. Jim asked me lots of questions, mostly about the core beliefs I'd formed as a child. Though an interesting journey, deep down, I couldn't believe this questioning could make a difference.

Upon leaving their home, I asked Jim what I should do next, and he said simply: you will be fine now. How could it be that simple? After all, I had tried so many times in so many ways for nearly four years for this to stop. I couldn't quite get my head around how this addiction could be over forever.

Sure enough, it wasn't, and for the next few days, the behaviour actually intensified. Anyone who has ever struggled with addiction will know the despair and hopelessness that comes with such a challenge. I had tried everything and had nothing left; I had nowhere else to turn. Exhausted and depleted, I felt like I had to give up and accept this as a permanent part of my life, and that's exactly what happened next. I gave up trying to run from this awful monster. Shortly after this darkest moment of my life, I prayed again: "Dear God, please help me. I'm on my hands and knees. If I can be cured, I'm ready, and if not, I will learn to cope with it."

Soon thereafter, I realised I had fallen into the fire of surrender for the second time in my life.

I remember, clearly, how an inner peace and acceptance filled my body. I had put my life into the hands of God. A long, long time had passed since I had felt any peace. Definitely, something had changed. Over the next few days, I noticed even though the bingeing/purging behaviour still occurred, the anxiety associated with it had fallen away. My brain told me no more stories about it, as if I simply witnessed my actions without any judgment.

The next week, Jim's partner, Elly, phoned me and asked how it was going. I reported the behaviour had not stopped, but I had noticed something had changed. I'd accepted this would be my fate and no one could help me, so I couldn't see any point in going back to work with Jim again. After I'd thanked her for her concern, I moved to hang up, when Elly pleaded with me to go back for another session. In spite of my resistance, I found myself saying yes and booking another appointment.

Reluctantly, I arrived at their home feeling sceptical and with little hope of things changing. Somehow, I had gotten my body there, and that alone was surprising enough. This time Jim took me through a journey into parts of myself split off as a child and wove a pathway back to my wholeness. Elly was again taking notes and was more involved with this second session. The process revealed core beliefs that held me in their grip. They were so masterful and caring. Four hours later, I left feeling calm and peaceful.

On the drive home, I noticed the colours of the trees and sky looked brighter than I had experienced before. An awareness arose from deep within. My reality had shifted—something had fallen away while something else had awoken.

From that day (thirty-five-plus years ago), this addictive behaviour has never occurred again. No withdrawal. No anxiety. It seemed as if it had never happened. A four-year addiction that consumed my life had stopped abruptly, healed that day. My relationship to food had normalized. The impulse to the habit had collapsed, and I became free of it. A miracle had occurred. It took several months before I could relax properly and trust it had, in fact, healed. I grew so awestruck by the power of this process, Jim Tolchard became my mentor. I studied intensively with him for four years, learning how core beliefs and thinking affect us.

In one of our five-day intensive programs, Jim announced to the group that I was one of the biggest liars he had ever met. Stunned, I looked at him and the other participants for answers and especially solace. I prided myself in being an honest person. Besides, I believed myself the world's worst liar. A little later, I learned he wasn't talking about that. He didn't explain what he meant for three long days. I felt ashamed and deeply uncomfortable.

On the last day of the program, I got it! Suddenly, I realised all the times and ways I lied to myself and, as a result, to others. He saw the light bulb go on and said, "Yes, every time you abandon yourself and pretend everything is okay when it is not. You have played the hostess with the mostest role along with other roles, and none of them are who you are. You don't even know who you are."

Shortly after that awful experience, Jim conducted a meditation. The "me" I knew fell away, and I was overcome by a euphoric sense of oneness. It was a glimpse into my true nature. It was a space I had known as a child in nature and one I would seek to understand for a very long time.

In deep gratitude and with a desire to pay it forward, I worked with many young people who were either suicidal or addicted and feel grateful to have received guidance upon this path through my direct experience. Compassion awakened in me as I related to the struggle I heard in so many of their stories.

Healthier and able to continue working in my business, I set up a small office downtown and procured contracts to assist companies and individuals in a troubleshooting endeavour. I seemed to have quite a knack for identifying patterns and problems within the team and facilitating the solutions sourced directly from them. Also, I facilitated many public-speaking programs for companies in the corporate world. It provided a great basis of learning and money to make ends meet.

Parallel to this, I felt a deeper connection to an intrinsic guidance, and even though I couldn't speak of such things in the business world in the 80s, my trust in something greater than myself developed. A deep pool of silence stirred inside my whole being. I knew with certainty something so powerful would come next, and I had no idea it would be living in a quaint treehouse on a small Island in the Pacific Ocean. A future with the most precious soul joining my life, conceived at the treehouse.

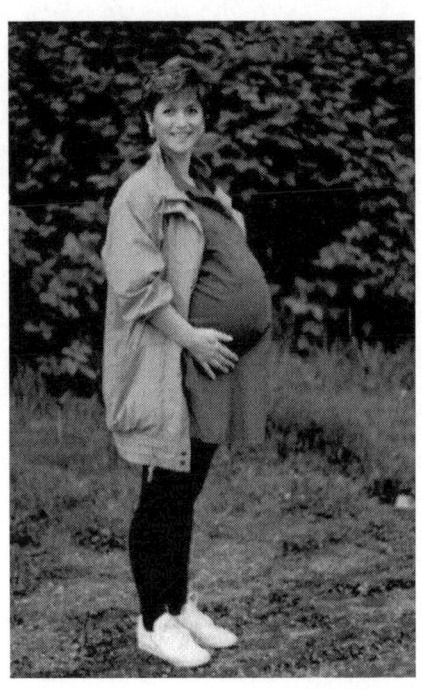

Chapter Five

THE HAND OF DESTINY

She whispered from the Tree House
Destiny had been set
It was purer than a flower
Old as a stone

On May 22, 1987, on a gorgeous sunny day with blue skies, my beautiful baby girl was born. She was a tenacious and curious spirit I would need a village to raise and who would one day become an equine veterinarian and my horse hero.

As the joy of being a mother blossomed, the gap between me and my husband got bigger, yet I know our hearts loved each other deeply. I guess the love wasn't enough to make things work.

I knew our marriage was in trouble before getting pregnant and this became increasingly obvious as he distanced himself with his work.

I could tell my husband was deeply troubled and carried unresolved conflicts and secrets. At the time, I was too afraid to ask him.

Finally, when he didn't come home at night, I confronted him. I sensed deeply that something was going on beyond what he was admitting. He called me jealous and over-reacting. My confidence sank, and I doubted myself, thinking I was crazy.

I didn't know the extent of what he was up to. I knew for sure he had had a number of affairs, including one with my maid of honour the week before we got married. I didn't find out the truth about this for a couple of years, until she had been drinking one night with me and couldn't hold on to her secret any longer, begging me for forgiveness. I told her I suspected it all along but didn't want to face the truth a few days before my wedding. My body and soul knew the truth, but I allowed my mind to over-ride it. I forgave her quickly based on the circumstances she spoke of but the friendship ended the day she confessed.

To add insult to injury, I learned he was involved in drugs and some kind of illegal exploits. There were many dark secrets I did not know the details of, and when I look back on this period of my life, I see I was in so much denial. I had normalized the things going on around me because I didn't understand the magnitude of crime involved.

I desperately wanted to leave but had locked myself in a golden cage, lying in so many ways. I didn't even know what these lies were, but I could feel them in my body and in the air, especially now Jim had so vividly pointed them out to me. My husband insisted I had nothing to worry about, and I pretended everything was okay on the outside, but on the inside, I was preparing my exit and made my intentions perfectly clear to him.

It was the weekend my husband was away at a Corvette rally he attended every year. Before he left, I pointed to the large boxes on the stairwell. They had been there for a few weeks as I was plucking up courage to leave. He knew it was in the works. I told him I would be leaving while he was gone, and the only thing he said as he was walking out the door was, "If you're leaving before I return, make sure you feed the dogs."

Unfortunately, I was not able to take my two dogs, Gina, a sweet St. Bernard, and Berti, a handsome black Great Dane. I had raised and loved them since they were puppies. It broke my heart not to take them with me, but survival was my number-one concern and I had to stay strong. I made a promise, as I was walking out the door, to come and get them as soon as I was on my feet again.

It was a terrifying day. I was scared and felt raw and vulnerable, leaving what appeared to be security and wealth behind. It wasn't just myself I had to look out for; I had a small baby and no money, just a song and a prayer. But in the end, it was for her that I found the courage to leave.

My husband would be getting back from his trip on Sunday evening, and after securing my baby in our rented apartment in the care of Chrystalle, I went back to the house to be there when he got home. I knew it wasn't going to be pretty but felt compelled to be there when he returned. I should not have cared at all but instead felt sorry for him.

I was scared of what might happen, but I was ready to meet his anger or rage or tears.

He walked through the door and saw me sitting there looking pensive. Glancing around the room, he could see the furniture had been rearranged. I had taken some furniture but left enough for him to still have a home as well. I left him the full bedroom suite, and the living room and dining room furniture. I felt justified in taking the large settee that I had recently purchased from the proceeds of a talk I gave. I took most of my daughter's things and her bedroom furniture. I left the kitchen intact and took just a few things to get us by.

He was shocked because he didn't think I would actually leave in spite of me telling him I was going to. He was furious as he stomped around the place, throwing a pan at the wall and threatening me with lawyers. Then he became more subdued and wanted to know my address. I didn't tell him right away but assured him I would as soon as we were settled, and within the first week I gave him the address and he came over to visit us.

Living in an apartment in Vancouver with my baby was a relief on one hand, but I was deeply sad and scared. The separation and uncertainty ripped at my heart. I remember wondering if I would ever feel happy again.

Although clearly our marriage was over, my husband was devoted to our daughter and staying in her life. After a few weeks, once we got settled in, he started regular visits. And I must say, in her presence, we always treated each other kindly. He loved his little girl fiercely and played on the floor with her throughout his entire visits. Eventually he would take her for some of the weekends. Although I was always cautious and worried until she returned, I was under a court order to let him take her.

Many months later, I returned to the farmhouse to meet with him to discuss some legal matters. I decided to go alone, knowing the conversations may be heated. Pulling into the driveway of the house I didn't see my dogs and wondered where they were since they were always outside and would run and greet me. I figured they must be in the house. I missed them so much and still intended to bring them with me as soon as I found a place that allowed dogs.

And then I found out the devastating news; my two beloved dogs had been poisoned.

At first, I thought it must have been some kind of accident and they got into some poison at the barn or something but I quickly found out what actually happened. They had been killed as a threat to my husband, should he share information with the police about names he had regarding a drug cartel. I found out our home phone lines had been under police surveillance for a year. All this was news to me, and I started to understand the severity of the problem.

How could anyone have deliberately done this to innocent and precious dogs? And now I knew the stark reality of the position we were in.

He too was sad about the situation and showed me the place he had buried them beside the house. He never disclosed the names of the people involved or the trouble he was in. I felt an undercurrent of fear, but I never told anyone or tried to get help. I was too afraid of what might happen. He did tell me to be cautious and not to go out at night on the porch with our daughter, since this threat was very real and they were now threatening to harm his wife and baby's life.

I drove away and had to pull over on the freeway because I couldn't see the road through the tears. I wept intensely for my precious dogs. And I wept for the entire mess my husband was in, feeling the uncertainty of my life, now as a single mother with a small child, and a threat hanging over our heads. I honestly didn't know if I would ever get over the magnitude of this loss. It was a gut-wrenching bind.

From then on, I stayed totally out of my husband's affairs and set up a separation agreement. It took nearly a year before I felt normal again, and fortunately nothing bad happened to us.

Then he surprised me by beginning his own healing journey and taking a six-month course involving a lot of deep emotional sessions and rebirthing as well as studying The Course in Miracles.[1]

I was duly impressed with him since it was not at all in his regular wheelhouse. He was a corporate guy with a scientific, conservative disposition. It gave me hope for our daughter that he was taking responsibility for his life waking up to a better way of being.

---

[1] The Course in Miracles – Dr.Helen Schucman

Chapter Six

VISION QUEST

The caterpillar calls it death
the Master calls it
transformation

Our daughter was three when the seeking to understand life and climb back into the silence was rekindled. I found some books and courses to quench my appetite as a spiritual seeker.

My husband had completed his program, and I became curious to learn more about it and signed up for the same course. Halfway through attending, I was faced with a big challenge. Part of the requirement of the program was to experience four days and nights alone. It didn't have to happen outside but did have to be isolated from our usual life. Right away I thought: If I'm going to do it, I would like to do a traditional vision quest, as I was drawn to the aboriginal teachings. I wanted to challenge my greatest fears, and this would be a powerful way to do it.

I was still scared of the dark, so the idea of doing a traditional vision quest brought up a lot of fear. To sit for four days and four nights high up on a mountain, all alone with no food and no tent was a challenging proposition.

A vision quest, as I learned through the Indigenous teachings, is something you do as a way of praying for a vision or, as it's traditionally referred to, crying for a vision. It forms a spiritual initiation and proves a powerful process. People told me you do not decide to do this lightly. It takes preparation and commitment.

So, it was quite the surprise to find myself on the edge of a difficult decision. *Will I do this, or will I not?* I remember, vividly, sorting through the fears about going. Why should I? I didn't have to. Or did I? My life appeared good; I was finally happy at home, had a wonderful, healthy child—why would I need to do this?

One good reason came from trying desperately to sort out my life: the struggle with my ex-husband had worn me down. I felt so confused and busy, I had lost sight once again of the inner stillness and truth.

My ego had a heyday, telling me if I did it, I would get murdered up there on the mountain or tortured by a bear or some other wild animal; that all kinds of strange and awful things could happen to me.

Nonetheless, a deep inner knowing emerged about the alignment of this vision quest, which enticed me forward. A patient but persistent movement stirred my soul. The experience involves solitude in a natural place, fasting to encourage emptiness, vulnerability through exposure to the elements and self-reliance to develop self-trust.

Early one morning, while sitting contemplating this over a cup of tea, I knew I had to do it. I had to obey this inner call. Somehow, I realised, at a deep level, this decision wasn't even mine to make. It was already made, and I was simply walking towards it. Even though the fear felt horrendous, and the ego was telling me I would die, in that moment, I knew it was that important and I truly would be willing to die for this if necessary.

As divine timing would have it, I was honoured to attend a sweat lodge a few weeks earlier with my group and met a man I thought could be my guide. I learned offering tobacco was customary and a sign of respect when requesting help. Pat, a First Nations elder and medicine man agreed to be my guide. He acted kindly, and I was humbled by the fact that he would do this for me even though I wasn't from his tradition. I shared with him my doubt about not being sanctioned to do this given the colour of my skin and the religion I was born into. He graciously reassured me that Creator doesn't care what colour skin you have, it is all about sincerity. He would use the term "All My Relations" in ceremonies and that said it all.

There were many questions I had to consider in preparing for this quest. He made it perfectly clear it was not a fad or game but a serious initiation.

My first obligation was to gather the materials to make medicine ties filled with tobacco. He asked me to do hundreds of them, which seemed daunting but important. I found colourful cotton fabric, as instructed, to represent the four directions. My guide told me to put my intentions and prayers into the tobacco as I secured the little bundles. I had to do this in a conscious and deliberate way. If I felt tired or angry, I needed to stop and clear the emotions before continuing. Only the purest of thought should go into them.

What on the surface seemed like an easy task turned into a major workout for me. It took hours every day for a week, mostly because of all the internal chatter and fear going on in my mind. I had to keep stopping to release fear or frustration. It became such a powerful process, as it made me painfully aware of the thoughts and feelings running through my head in a way I hadn't noticed before. Also, I couldn't keep the little bundles from knotting together, since they were to be threaded continuously, totalling approximately fifty feet. Apparently, this would provide the boundary and home

I would sit in for four days and nights, exposed to the elements, but supposedly safe within this sacred circle.

Chrystalle offered support by keeping my daughter entertained and fed while I struggled away to finish the task upstairs in my bedroom. It took me a week to complete, and already I had learned so much. I realised my vision quest had already begun.

My ex called me crazy, saying I didn't need to take the assignment this far. He did his four-day solo in a completely different way, staying in his truck and a small hut in the woods. Soon, though, his attitude transformed to admiration, and he supported and encouraged my decision. Later, he admitted staying outside for four days and nights wasn't something he could have done, and he said my courage amazed him.

Finally the day came when I made my way to the location of my vision quest. It took the better part of a day to arrive on this beautiful Gulf Island in the Strait of Georgia, British Columbia.

Day One of the Vision Quest

The Medicine Man escorted me up the mountain to the location he had carefully chosen. It was remote, and it made for quite a climb to a clearing overlooking the ocean in the distance. We both puffed our way up the narrow pathway until we reached the spot I would call my home for four days and nights. I had a small backpack with a few clothing items, a sleeping bag, a toothbrush, a tiny container of water and, of course, my large bundle of tobacco medicine ties.

Upon arrival, Pat asked me to get out the medicine ties and create a boundary. First, we had to find the four directions. We established East, and from there, I set about aligning the appropriate colours with the North, South, and West. He had also asked me to bring extra cotton fabric, which he used to place flags around the outside.

Under Pat's watchful eye, I opened my fat bundle of medicine ties, feeling a bit awkward and shy. I unwound them around the designated area, approximately twelve feet square. Partway through, the string and tobacco ties got caught in a knot, and the more I tried to unravel them, the worse it got. My cheeks blazed on fire, and I felt embarrassed. Eventually, Pat intervened and gave me a hand by cutting and re-tying them. I watched while he gracefully and silently fixed the medicine ties. He never said much, but when he did speak, I listened up. "I see your life's in a bit of a knot," he said.

I dropped my eyes in shame and agreed this was true. Part of the reason I'd embarked upon this program was the need to sort out the entanglement I had gotten into with my husband, who I had separated from a couple of years earlier, and my boyfriend. Even though I was completely and legally separated from my ex, a kind of triangle had formed with my boyfriend of over a year.

At last, we got all the ties freed and the circle and my boundary set. Seated in the circle together, I confessed to Pat I felt totally petrified of the dark and questioned whether I would manage to do this as planned. After listening to my concerns, he said he would put a man up on the hill close by for the first night.

Satisfied my "sacred space" had been set, he made his way down the trail. I sat wondering if there was anything else I should know, and I wanted to call out after him. Sensing this, he turned back and motioned that he would return soon. I assumed this included the "protector" he would bring me.

As a child, I loved nature and felt totally happy and safe in her enfold. I don't know why I became so afraid of the dark as an adult. I was alone on the mountain, with no food, nothing to read, nothing to write on, and no tent to hide in but just a small tarp, and it started raining. Pretty soon, it set to pouring down, and my heart sank. "What have I done? I've given up my life for this. What an idiot." I scurried around, trying to make a shelter with the piece of plastic Pat had allowed me to bring, but it barely covered me. I grew cold and damp. Boy, did I ever feel sorry for myself. I spent the afternoon trying to quiet my mind, but it ran out of control, especially fearing the inevitable darkness that would descend within the next couple of hours.

Dusk had arrived by the time I saw Pat coming toward me up the trail. He came alone, and my heart skipped a beat. He greeted me with a nod and informed me the grandfathers had said he should not leave a man up on the hill with me. Instead, he should give me his sacred pipe to smoke if I became afraid. I didn't realise at the time how great an honour this was. I wondered how smoking a pipe could bring any relief from the fear. He said to smoke the pipe and pray hard, and with no further explanation, left the mountain.

I wanted to call after him, "Please, take me with you. I cannot stay out here alone," but instead, I remained silent, watching him disappear. I grew angry with myself: what a vulnerable position I'd put myself in. I lost my connection to God and felt separate and alone. My ego had taken over completely.

Sad and frightened, I jumped into my sleeping bag and cried like a child wanting to go home desperately. Little did I know this formed the entire purpose of this quest. People called me courageous, but right then, I felt like a coward. As night drew near, the terror rising in my tummy became unbearable, and I thought I would throw up. The yakkidy-yak-yak mind never letting up for a second, and already I felt exhausted. The doubt drew images of all kinds of horrible things happening to me. The fear was mostly centred on never seeing my daughter again; I ached and missed her so much. Why had I sequestered myself from all that I trusted and loved?

Upon noticing the sacred pipe, I thought I'd give it a try and smoke it. "Yeah . . . right," said my ego. "As if that's going to help." I had never smoked a cigarette in my life and just about choked on the smoke when it entered my throat. The last thing I could remember was to pray hard—I felt pissed, and at that moment could not find any reverence at all for this sacred pipe. I put it aside and fell into a dark hole of despair. My body trembled with fear and cold.

Many times, I got up indignantly as if to call this whole thing off, but then felt myself receiving encouragement to lay back down. All kinds of scary noises reached me, making me wonder if this night were to be my demise. It was one of the scariest nights of my life. Not because I was actually in danger but because I had scared myself so violently.

How I got through that first night, I'll never know. I kept one eye open and begged for relief through sleep but to no avail. The night seemed endless and dark. But as soon as the first light betrayed the night, I relaxed and fell into a long and deep sleep.

Day Two of the Vision Quest

When I awoke, the sun shone brightly high in the sky, and I guessed it must be around noon. I worried how I would make it through another night, and another after that, and another. Every passing minute seemed like an eternity.

During the days, I tried to meditate and get into a state of peace, but of course, the harder I tried, the more it eluded me. I have never been a person to experience boredom, but I certainly felt the days elongate and extend beyond reason. My brain went over and over memories and future scenarios. I pined for my daughter and worried in case she missed me.

I prayed, but not yet sincerely . . ..

The possibility of an actual vision had crossed my mind a few times, but I didn't have any particular attachment to what this might be or how it might get delivered. My ego mind inferred that since I was not Indigenous, I didn't deserve to have a real vision. I was just fulfilling the requirements of my course.

The incessant mind was one thing, but the physical part was just as difficult. I was afraid the fasting part would precipitate a response from my previous eating disorder. I felt vulnerable and unstable but had nothing to eat anyway and only a small amount of water. The cravings were hard, and I kept telling my body we would eat again in a few days. As well I had to deal with a caffeine headache from stopping tea and coffee cold turkey.

For hours, I reflected upon my life, running over the many passages and setbacks and trying to make sense of it all: the mistakes I had made, the confusion I had ended up in, and the decisions yet to be handled. I tortured myself violently and critically. After all the personal development work I had done, and with supposedly growing so much—how could I have gotten back here again?

Day Three of the Vision Quest

On the third day, I knew a shift had occurred, but still I fought with myself about everything the mind projected onto my screen to take a look at. Joined with this was the dialogue explaining and judging why and how and why not I had done things the way I did. It was a thorough review process.

In the afternoon, I stood up quickly and started retching. Nothing much came up, just a little bit of water, but in a way, it felt like a metaphor of purging deep and painful emotions. At this point, I surrendered and became silent inside.

Soon I started to notice images but without the commentary. Instead, there was a sense of simply witnessing the movie without being involved, and a peace started moving into my body.

Every evening, at some point, Pat paid a quiet visit. He would check in from a distance and leave. This night, he came over and looked at me and said, "Ah, you've passed through the wall." He smiled and disappeared again. I had entered into such a place of peace, I was unsure whether he had actually come by or if I had imagined it.

Day Four of the Vision Quest

The next day, it dawned beautiful and sunny. My life had begun anew as I breathed in the fresh air and basked in the stillness. Until that day, it was so noisy inside, I couldn't hear the sound of silence or feel the presence of nature or the beauty surrounding me. The fear had obscured it all. Now, while I sat in such peace, I noticed my surroundings for the first time.

High up on a bluff, I could see the ocean in the distance. Eagles soared close up above, and hummingbirds and dragonflies spiralled around me. Deer roamed nearby and seemed undisturbed by my presence. Suddenly, I realised some of the sounds that had so alarmed me at night had come from the deer grazing nearby.

Standing up and looking out, I spotted a beautiful big monarch butterfly way down below on a jagged ridge. It looked gorgeous, and I invited it to come closer. In utter amazement, I watched it fly gracefully toward me. Delight filled my body when it came closer and closer. Soon, it landed on my right shoulder, and I stood spellbound. My heart opened, and tears of pure joy filled my eyes. I felt God's presence and such deep gratitude for the first time on this quest. The Indigenous people say certain animals in nature are symbolic for us, and we are to pay attention. The butterfly is about transformation, and I had transformed, and this gave me a symbol. Reminiscent of the treehouse days, I was at home sitting in stillness. I felt like I could stay forever.

Pat had encouraged me to stay awake during the last night on the hill, which I was able to for most of it. I felt calm, at peace, and free. What a major contrast from my first night.

In the morning, while waiting for Pat to come and escort me back down, I found myself building a fire. He said I could do this, but up until then, I hadn't for two reasons. Firstly, I didn't want to attract attention to where I was, and secondly, I didn't know how to. Embarrassed at never having built a fire in my whole life, I thought, *what if I can't do it?'* At which point I exploded with laughter. As if anyone lingered around to see but me. And so, I set about building my fire.

Sure enough, I built a roaring fire and crouched beside it in awe of its power. After I rose and stepped back from it, I became dizzy. Fainting, I fell backward to the ground. I'm sure I was out for only seconds.

Soon, I opened my eyes and sat up. In that moment I saw an amazing image, multi-dimensional, suspended right in front of me, much like a hologram. It was of a human baby being regurgitated out of an eagle's mouth. The baby looked robust and healthy, and not at all traumatized from having come out of the eagle's mouth.

I sat riveted in stillness as I watched this beautiful imagery at the edge of my eyes. *Oh, my God . . .* I suddenly realised this must be the vision about which Indigenous people speak.

Later that day, Pat came to escort me down from the mountain and could tell I felt happy and pleased with myself for having completed my vision quest. Traditionally, after such a quest, it is important to go into the sweat lodge to complete the experience. Pat had prepared this for me, and it awaited my arrival. As I made my way down the hillside, I became aware I carried a far lighter load than the burdened emotional luggage I had packed up there. A feeling of elation hit me, mixed with a little sadness at leaving my "safe space" behind. It had become my cocoon and place of transformation. It also made for the beginning of learning this sacred space, this sanctuary, lay within me and I now knew how to access it.

The sweat lodge was excruciatingly hot, and I didn't feel strong enough to handle it as I crawled into the womb-like structure. It was a final ceremony to give thanks to the grandfathers and grandmothers for watching over me and helping me to interpret the vision. Pat said it surprised and pleased him that I had completed the vision quest. He hadn't thought I would make it, given my level of fear in the beginning. As for the vision, he said I carried Eagle medicine. He spoke about how it's our parent's role to raise us to a certain age until we can make decisions for ourselves. He said the problem is many continue mistakenly making decisions based on this past programming, which no longer serves us. He told me this image symbolized the re-birthing of myself and making decisions from a new understanding, and now my instructions would come from the Great Mother and Great Father of the Earth and Sky, from Creator.

It made sense, as I listened to his words, and I knew its meaning would deepen in time. I felt blessed to have received a vision, the last thing I had expected. My focus had lain mostly on getting through the vestiges of the ego.

Pat also said I shouldn't share this vision for at least a year. I crawled from the sweat lodge to the nearby house. Though I felt happy, my body was so weak. I guessed correctly that the lack of energy came from the combination of fasting and the emotional release. Indeed, after a delicious bowl of miso soup and a good hot shower, the energy bounced right back. Pretty soon, I set off on my way home. Or, should I say, I had reached home already and now went to where I lived.

On the drive, I reflected back to the terror I had experienced at the beginning of this quest. Truly, I had gone through the fire and, like the phoenix, risen out of the ashes four days later.

This foreshadowed my work with silence and nature and honouring my calling. Nature and silence are where you will find your answers and awakenings.

Over the following years I learned much about the plight of the Indigenous people in Canada and the US and deeply honour the teachings I experienced from these traditions. This spirituality spoke to my heart with my love of nature and the understanding that we are all connected. All My Relations.

Chapter Seven

OBEDIENCE

*When the phone rings
you do not have to
answer it
When spirit calls
you do*

Two and a Half Years Later.

I was in a wonderful relationship with Ron, a man I had known since coming to Canada. We were both working at CJOR radio station and had dated for well over a year and a half at this point. I felt deeply connected to him and happy. Our souls resonated and we shared much creativity and fun together. My daughter loved him, and he loved and treated her kindly.

One day we were reading out loud, the book Never Cry Wolf by Farley Mowat and Ron commented that I reminded him of Angeline, the female wolf in the story. Before reaching the end of the book he started calling me Angeline as a kind of nick name and I felt a resonance right away as I met the sound of this name coming towards me. I liked it and it felt real. And pretty much from that point forth I knew this was my name. I asked family members and friends to call me by the name Angelyn. It took years before they would really get behind it but after a while they did. In the early 90's I legalized my name change and modified the spelling to Angelyn. Cool, my boyfriend had given me my new name.

Then the craziest thing happened. At what turned out to be a pivotal point in my life, I was asked to do something that made no sense to me at all; something in which I had no interest. In fact, it seemed like an insane idea.

I had never been good at obedience in the traditional sense of the word. I didn't like rules and was quite undisciplined in certain areas of my life, but when I got instructions from this deep, deep place inside, I have only one choice—*obedience*. And here is where the true meaning of Radical Trust took hold within me.

The beginning of my ability to hear guidance as kind of a whisper came on a trip I took with Ron to Oregon. It was different than at the treehouse where guided words tumbled through my fingers onto the computer. This was like I could hear something at an ultrasonic range, like a dog hears a high-pitched whistle.

It was a weeklong retreat at a place called Breitenbush. One day, while hiking out by the hot springs, I heard the whisper for the first time. It said, "*You have to go back with your husband.*" It bothered me, and I thought for sure I was making it up.

Throughout the rest of the retreat, it happened several times. The message came in a kind of quiet undertone, patient, and without any overt pressure, but definitely very clear. I didn't want to disturb the repose of our time away, so I opted not to share it with Ron.

Sitting in the hot springs, I did contemplate its meaning. Why would I be asked to do this? My ex-husband and I co-parented well, and I couldn't imagine a reason to go back. Perhaps it was about completing the relationship with him and getting on with the divorce. Altogether, it seemed bizarre; I had not the slightest bit of interest in doing it.

After we left Breitenbush, the gentle nudging continued. *Go back with your husband,* it repeated. No way, I thought, and dismissed it as a ridiculous idea.

Eventually, the inner stirring became so insistent I had to consider it until, finally, reluctantly, I obeyed the message. I didn't speak with my husband first to see if he was even open to the idea but felt pretty certain he would agree.

Instead, I wanted to sit down with my boyfriend and explain what was going on for me and what I had been struggling with. We arranged to have lunch at our favourite restaurant, the Naam, a funky old vegetarian restaurant that's been around for decades, originating out of the hippie era.

I was already waiting there at the restaurant when Ron walked in and joined me. He was looking a little concerned, and I remember feeling this laughter welling up at the ridiculousness of what I planned to share, or maybe I was reacting to some fear surfacing in my body.

Barely before he sat down I blurted out, "I have to go back with my husband." I was nervous and knew this was going to upset him.

He sat still, looking at me intensely. "What?" he asked.

"I know this sounds strange, but I keep receiving intuitive guidance about this, and it feels important."

"Yes, I know. You got the message at Breitenbush, didn't you?"

Wow, this surprised me. "How do you know?"

"Because I got it too. But you don't have to follow it," he said.

Yes, but I do, came the whisper from my heart and soul.

We had lunch together, but it felt tense and sad at the thought of letting go of each other. He couldn't understand why I would listen to this message and act upon it. After all, didn't I have free will? I told him I couldn't explain it and definitely didn't like it, but I had to be obedient to this.

He was not so understanding at the time, and I don't blame him, even I thought the idea of going back was absurd.

Over the next few days, I considered deeply what was being asked of me. Could I do it? How could I let go of Ron? He was my beloved partner and playmate. If I went back, I couldn't pretend just for the sake of it. I would have to leap in with both feet and let go of Ron completely. I could only do this with utmost integrity.

When I asked my ex-husband, the following week, what he thought of this, he responded happily and excited. It was what he had hoped for, to bring the family back together again. So, I went against my mind that screamed, "What are you doing? You're crazy. It's a big mistake." All I had was a deep knowing about it that was impossible to explain.

Many of my friends thought I'd lost my mind, and some wouldn't speak to me, saying I was sabotaging my life and making an awful mistake. Chrystalle was the only one asking, "How can I support you?"

I didn't want to go ahead, but that inner knowing led me forward and soon arrangements were made for my husband to move into my house in Vancouver.

To show my commitment, I agreed to take his legal name and became a Toth. When we got married, I had kept my maiden name (Elliott), so this was my way of proving how all-in I was. I fixed up the bedroom and, in all sincerity and willingness, I put my heart and soul into it.

The first few nights, we anchored ourselves on opposite sides of the bed, and it felt awkward as hell. I'd fall asleep at night remembering the old feelings left over from our marriage, wondering what in God's name I had done. I tried desperately for it to work out, but I felt hopeless with so many painful memories resurfacing. It felt impossible for us to become intimate in spite of good intentions. We tried to use the tools we had learned, and I remember many a "clearing" upstairs with us sitting opposite each other in upright chairs and sharing how we felt. It proved to be a bottomless pit of stuff to work through, though relief did come, for a short while, after the clearing.

The task of sewing together a frayed relationship was unbelievably difficult and attempting to do so made no sense to me. It ripped at my soul because I didn't understand why my inner voice had led me back. It didn't feel good, and the same problems were happening all over again. What was I thinking? I continued hoping things would get better. After all, I had uprooted my daughter, let go of my partner and wanted to see if it was possible to be a family once again. Not one to give up easily, I persisted on.

As our daughter was getting close to her fifth birthday, I started remembering the message I had received at the treehouse in 1986: *this being (baby) was coming in for five years.* But what did this mean? Was she going to die soon? I tried to dismiss it as foolish and superstitious, but it did worry me.

One evening after dinner, my husband and I went for a walk for some one-on-one time. We were walking alongside the beach when it felt like a good time to share my concern. I told him of the message I had received about our daughter coming to be with us for five years and how here she was on the brink of her fifth birthday. I said it was probably nonsense, but I needed to share it with him because I was beginning to panic.

His reaction startled me. He fell to the ground and rolled back and forth in the fetal position, repeating quietly, "Oh, my God. Oh, no. Oh, no." I panicked because he was not typically demonstrative. I sensed the seriousness of this, and it worried me even more.

Over the next few weeks, we lived on edge as her fifth birthday came and went. We did our best to put it out of our minds.

As well, our relating was difficult, and it didn't feel like we had made any progress. Within two weeks of moving back in together, he ended up having an affair with a woman he'd previously dated (I sensed it, but I didn't know the truth until way later).

As a small child, my husband lived through a traumatic life event as he and his family escaped Hungary in 1956 during the Revolution. Cold and afraid for their lives, his father led them through the bleak night, with soldiers on watch, across the border to Austria. The reason I share this is I know it impacted him greatly and he was only just beginning to unravel this trauma through baby steps on his healing journey, or perhaps I'm just trying to understand it.

After enduring three months of trying to make our relationship work, I felt terrible about having gone back with my husband. What had I done? What a mistake. I had disrupted everybody's lives to do this but just couldn't penetrate the steel wall standing between us. We couldn't let each other's love in.

I prayed every night for answers. What was the point of this? What piece was I missing? *Dear God, help me to make this easier. I want to let his love in, but I don't trust. Help*

me get beyond my fear so I can see our innocence once again.
Help me see what and why I was asked to go back. It became a
most difficult time for us all.

The next day, sitting in the local Muffin Break having a
latte and muffin, I felt unhappy and miserable. The
feeling continued as I made my way out to my car. I had
barely driven out of the parking lot when this rap song
came pouring through me. I pulled the car over and
scribbled down the words as fast as they came tumbling
out.

<u>New Attitude</u>
I'm tired of all the eating
I'm tired of getting fat
I'm tired of always hearing
yakkidy-yak-yak
I'm tired of feeling awful
I'm tired of all the pain
I'm tired of all the doubt and
I'm tired of all the shame
This right here is the end of the line
I ain't taking it one more time
all the tired feelings
all the victim's stuff
all the shallow ceilings
and all the old guff
Pile 'em all together

put gasoline over top
strike a match of fire
and burn the bloody lot
I'm cleaning up my act now
it's gonna change today
I don't have to live my life this way
Instead, I deserve abundance today
love in my life and warm sunny days
I give up the struggle officially today
from now on, I'm only willing to play
Playing's my game; I'm gonna have some fun
I'll act as if my life just begun
'cept I'm doing the choosing of what I believe
I'm doing the creating of whatever I please
so bye, bye to old, hi to the new
from now on, I have a new attitude
Bye to the old. Hi to the new
from now on, I have a new attitude
Bye to the old. Hi to the new
from now on, I have a new attitude.

As I sat there pulled over, with the engine still running, I laughed at the words scrawling onto the page, with the rap song resounding in my head.

Afterwards, I received a further message: I could let go again.

What? Let go of *what?*

The marriage, came the indication.

I was flabbergasted. What did all this mean? I couldn't understand why I had been asked to go back for only three months, when clearly a reconciliation had not occurred. I started to doubt my intuition. I wondered if it had been a mistake all along. It pained me to uproot my daughter once more, especially when my friends and family hadn't believed it a good idea in the first place. The whole thing felt totally irrational, to put it mildly, but I followed this instruction from the deep place within and let go of my marriage one more time.

What surprised me was I didn't hear any resistance from the deep all-knowing part of myself. In fact, I got a clear message: *You can let go now.* It seemed as if I had just emerged from a major test of some kind. I still didn't know what the purpose of going back with my husband meant. I felt guilty and confused, berating myself for not interpreting my intuition clearly. Surely, I wouldn't have been asked to let go of a wonderful relationship to go back just for three months? The release felt so powerful, I wondered about it for a long time.

It would take a full year before I knew why I had to go back. After some drama and legal threats, my husband said he was going to fight for custody of our daughter and made sure I knew he had all the money in the world and as such would win the case. Having no money myself, I was petrified of losing my daughter. He hired an expensive and ruthless downtown lawyer, and I thought I was doomed.

Then one day this courage welled up from within and I approached him, saying: "We are not going to fight and spend a fortune on lawyers; instead we are going to go to the stone circle at Spanish Banks and sit down together, just the two of us, and hash out every detail of our separation agreement. We'll stay there until it is done, and only then will we take it to a lawyer to implement." I was a little shocked by the commanding

> *Thunder crashes*
> *throwing open the door*
> *They can speak now*

energy arising through my body as I made this proclamation. In a million years, I never could imagine him taking me up on this idea. A stone circle, what? To my absolute surprise, he agreed.

The following week we arrived at the stone circle and sat down in the centre and began the process of hashing out every detail and the steps needed to come to consensus. We spent quite a few hours there, arguing back and forth until finally, we reached agreement on every issue.

From there we worked with a lawyer to draw out our plan, and I was relieved we didn't have to go into a legal battle. I also understood that his "secret activities" were still going on, and I was in the dark about what they were but relieved to be away from them.

After the dust settled, I got on with rebuilding my life with the new circumstances I found myself in.

One day I literally ran into Ron at Granville Island and we reconnected. I was grateful he was still open to continuing with our relationship. Uncertain of what the whole process of me going back meant, we decided to put it in the past and move forward. The short version of the story is we decided to take a big leap of faith and bought a beautiful ocean-view home on Bowen Island, fulfilling a dream.

My ex could have caused problems about us leaving the mainland to live on Bowen Island but actually he felt it safer for us to be away from the Vancouver area due to continued threats he was receiving.

We did the best we could to communicate well for the sake of our daughter and he took her on alternate weekends for the first while, but it freaked me out what might happen given the threats he told me about. There were times she didn't want to go, and in spite of attempts to get help, I was in contempt of court if I didn't make her go. I learned a lot about the ridiculousness of the court system; until something bad happens they will not take the threats seriously.

I know he loved his daughter and would fight like a lion to protect her if necessary, but his problems proved insurmountable.

I didn't see him for a number of months after that, and then out of the blue he phoned and invited me to meet him in Horseshoe Bay. He had just returned from a business trip in Japan and wanted to see his daughter and give her a present. We had lunch together in the park and as promised, he gave her some presents, which was one of his most favourite things to do. It was his love language. He was so happy to see her, and having me at her side, she was happy to see him as well. He also gave me a little present in an envelope. It was the CD *Pretty Woman,* along with a beautiful card about relationship. In the card, he asked me to listen to track 9, "Fallen." It would take me years before I could actually listen to that track all the way through without crying. It speaks of how lost he was without me. My heart was ripped from the memories of our love and why it had been so complicated.

Over the prior year, things had been deeply strained between us, with problems and custody issues. It was a very difficult time for us all. Yet here he was, larger than life, looking happier and healthier than I had seen him in years. I guessed the trip to Japan must have been very good for him. And I was pleased.

Sitting on the blanket with our picnic in the park felt sweet as we watched our daughter playing happily on the swings. There was a warm breeze and blue skies lifting our spirits. The love radiated between the three of us, unencumbered by all the old stuff. This made for a special moment between us; it felt real and vulnerable. Pure and sweet. I'll never forget it because it was the last time I saw him alive. Three days later, at forty-one, he died of heart failure. The true details of his death, I will never really know. **He died in our daughter's fifth year.**

Chapter Eight

WHAT YOU TAKE WITH YOU

Caught in the eye of the hurricane
the roots bearing down
there's nothing to grab on to
Nothing

 Nothing could have prepared me for the phone call I received from my sister-in-law. She just came right out with it, **Steve is Dead.**

My brain couldn't make sense of what she said. I kept grabbing at variable ideas. *He's in hospital? He's sick? He had an accident.* I begged. And, scraping the barrel, my mind asked, *He's in jail?*

No, he's gone. He is dead, she replied.

How? What happened? I have to go and find him.

She said the coroner would not let anyone see him. I blurted out: *But I'm his wife.* She repeated that no one including me, was allowed to see him since he had been dead for 3 days before he was found, and his body had already been identified.

Panic ensued, and I could hardly breathe or hear her response. After hanging up, I ran outside, letting out a primal wail that must have rattled the heavens or, at the very least, startled the neighbours. Ron ran down to the beach where my daughter was playing with a friend and her mother. He asked if she could keep her for the day and he would pick her up later.

I tried to reach Chrystalle, but this was before the days of everyone having a cell phone, so I had her paged at the Vancouver Folk Festival where she had gone for the day. She called me as soon as she got the message and came straight back to Bowen to be with us. Next, I needed to talk to my dad. Upon hearing my voice, dad wanted to jump on a plane from England to support me. Feeling confused and shocked, I didn't know what to do, but it helped having his love on the other end of the phone. My friend Ariel came over as well and told us what to do and when to do it, because I couldn't think properly. Ariel is another earth angel who came into my life in a significant way, and we recognized each other as soul sisters the first time we met.

Words cannot describe the agony of this loss, and then worst of all, somehow, I had to face telling my little girl the devastating news. How was I ever going to do this?

Ron went to pick up my daughter late that evening and brought her back from the neighbour's. As she walked through the door, she asked if we were still going to camp out in the rock room, as we had planned to do earlier that day. The rock room was a basement space where we had built a little camp-out nest in the rock cavity exposed into the room.

Ariel had warned me not to tell my daughter about her dad until the morning. She had had the misfortune of being told about her brother's death in the middle of the night, and it has caused distress throughout her life. I railed against it because I didn't think I could handle the waiting and pretending. In the end, I followed instruction and took my daughter to the rock room for our campout. I don't know how it happened, but in no time, she'd fallen fast asleep.

Wandering out onto the deck, I felt the warm wind blowing across the ocean, through my hair and touching my skin, bringing me into my body a little more. I felt the penetrating ache of despair and begged for this to be a bad nightmare when I woke up. The rest of the night I hovered over my child, rehearsing how I would tell her.

At 7:30 a.m., my little girl stirred and looked at me. She could tell something was wrong from the grief on my face and the fact I was fully alert and waiting. To tell my beloved daughter her daddy had died was the hardest thing I'd ever had to do. My grief and shock were compounded by the pain in my daughter's eyes. "You mean, I'll never see Daddy again?"

It was too soon, for her and for me, to teach how he would live on, in her heart. "No, baby, Daddy is gone." I recall mentioning something like, "Daddy is in heaven with God."

Grief stricken, we stayed in the rock room downstairs for a long time, just crying and holding each other. If not for Ron and my precious friends, we probably wouldn't have eaten for a week because the shock was immobilizing.

When I reflected on the order of things, it started to make sense why I couldn't find him. For three days, I had attempted to find him by phone, and he had a cell phone. It was his weekend to take our daughter, and he had promised to take her to the Vancouver Folk Festival. It was unlike him to be unreachable. He always picked up his phone, so I had been wondering why he wasn't, but not suspecting he had died. Ariel said she knew he had died, and it must have been because she's psychic or I had missed some serious cues (I was in so much denial).

It also struck me how he had died when our daughter reached five, and how clear this premonition was. As you can imagine, this unhinged me greatly, and months later, I sought counsel from Pat, the native elder who guided me on my vision quest. He helped me understand why I had received this message in the treehouse about her coming for five years. He said this being came to serve her father for the first five years of her life. She came to open his heart. After that, her path was about her own journey and growth. It had nothing to do with her dying, but about the job her soul had agreed to do.

And I witnessed the success of this. Her dad was a workaholic, and the only time I ever saw him put his work down was when his little girl walked into his home office. The switch happened immediately, and he gave her his total attention. He gave her priority, no matter what. His heart burst wide open with love for her, and she spent the first five years of her life being carried around by him whenever she was in his care.

But now he was gone, and I didn't know what I would have to deal with, since we were not even divorced. I dreaded the worst and suspected I would be left with some serious debt.

The opposite happened.

As my life lay in rubble, an insurance company informed me I had now become a wealthy woman, being left insurance money I had no idea would come to me. It was a great deal of money, and it began with a half-a-million-dollar insurance cheque that arrived by courier within days of my husband's death.

We had already separated our financial assets, and I didn't know what my financial responsibility would be by still being legally married.

When I found out about the amount of money coming to me, I felt faint and like I was having a panic attack. Ron was away from the house, so I called my neighbour to come over and sit with me while I tried to sort through my fears. She helped me relax and encouraged me to trust that everything would work out okay. I noticed how afraid of this I felt, thinking I would surely die. Images of leaving my daughter an orphan tormented me. How crazy it was, watching my mind translate this money to mean my demise or my daughter being kidnapped for the money. Having this much money scared the life out of me.

It was all too much to process at a time of grieving. I'm sure it was meant to bring some relief at this difficult time, but somehow it felt slightly off to be receiving a cheque before I had barely caught my breath from the shock of my husband's death. On the other hand, the efficiency of the insurance company was commendable.

Learning how to have money became a step-by-step enduring process. It brought an enormous responsibility. People have said to me they wish they had that kind of problem, and I always smiled because until you get faced with such a situation, you don't know what it will feel like. I was about to learn some of my toughest, darkest lessons, along with some of my greatest dreams coming true.

Not only did I live in fear, but I knew nothing about investment strategies and what to do with large sums of money. I didn't know whom I could trust, and I had tons of negative programming around money and rich people. It never ceases to amaze me the games the mind plays and how, at vulnerable times, the ego can get a strong hold.

The other shattering thing that happened was I severed my relationship with Ron. I believe the guilt of my husband dying and leaving me such an inheritance and, of course, the shock, destroyed my judgment. There was a two-week period I have no recollection of, but apparently, I was nasty and destructive.

Not feeling like I deserved to feel happy ever again carried a heavy toll. I don't know why my mind distorted his death to be my fault, but that's what happened. I wished I had been saner at the time, but shock distorts reality. It was emotionally violent for all involved. I did feel tremendous guilt about the tragedy my precious child had to endure. Losing two significant males in her life in the space of a few months was devasting.

After my husband died, I started taking care of the details of my life, including fulfilling the role as executor of his estate. The first thing I did was go out to his house to bring back my child's toys and clothes.

It was a tentative drive as I made my way towards his house, which was the house he had just died in. As I turned the corner, I saw his Bronco truck patiently waiting in his driveway like a loyal dog. Feeling shaky, I turned the key into the garage and entered.

Inside by the door were his sneakers, which I had seen many times before. They stopped me dead in my tracks and it struck me deep – his shoes were still there. I was surprised, as if he was supposed to have donned his shoes and left by the front door. There were other shoes lined up at the door, including our little girl's pink boots. Tears filled my eyes and my heart hurt.

His primrose 1958 Corvette elegantly stood in his carpeted garage, exactly how I had seen it last. A companion to this was his brand-new billiard table with his jacket thrown on it, along with scores from the last game. For years he had wanted a pool table, and I contemplated what a short lifespan they'd had together.

I entered his house and walked into the kitchen, which is where he left his body. Tapping into the energy of the room, it felt eerie and chaotic, as if his spirit was still trapped there.

His wallet and keys sat on the counter. Two of his shirts draped over the back of the kitchen chairs. I picked them up and smelled them, somehow hoping to make him real again. Looking around at all his things, I half expected him to come waltzing into the room any moment. Building images in my mind, I kept recreating him as if to change this present reality. But soon the hard truth hit – he was gone. He, the mortal person, no longer existed, but his immortal spirit lingered on.

So, what had these past years all been about, I questioned myself deeply. All the secrets and lies, hell bent on his quest to acquire wealth at any cost. He was frugal with himself, driven to succeed and never giving himself any time off or rewards along the way until the last few months of his life when things suddenly changed.

I looked around to see all his newly acquired luxurious furnishings, tastefully positioned in his new show house. Robert Bateman paintings covered the walls. He was just back from Japan, bringing jewellery and art and monogramed clothing and on and on and on . . . all these things he would never have bought before. I shuddered at how I acted impressed while he showed me his latest acquisitions. He never shared what he loved about the piece, only the price tag. Anger stirred momentarily within me as I realized my part in his script.

His business was already successful, but it was never enough. He never felt successful. He had achieved his lifelong goal of being a millionaire at forty, and part of the evidence sat around me. But at what price, and was it worth it?

Pictures that our little girl had painted for her daddy were taped over the fireplace, and sadness filled me as I remembered her trying to give him her art gifts. He looked at them for a second with no real awareness and proceeded to give her another gift he brought back from Japan. One gift after another; it felt so indulgent, and he never saw the disappointment on his little girl's face as he pushed her art aside and offered her another gift. All she wanted to do was give her daddy the picture she had painted for him. He mistakenly thought love was about giving her more gifts. If only he understood that receiving was also a gift.

With a deep sigh and memories of his face, I softened and remembered his gentleness. I could feel the deep love I still felt for him and the pain of what could have been ripped at my heart.

In his compulsion to succeed, he got tangled up in props to hold him up and keep him going – props that finally took his life.

And now I stood there in his kitchen and I ached in my heart for this man driven to succeed. Goals now sat around me limp with lifelessness, things that would soon be dispersed in all directions to people that may or may not really care. I ached inside, feeling further abandoned by him. I felt angry that he had left me to explain this to our little girl. Try telling a five-year-old her daddy is gone. If only he could have asked for help. "If only's" scrambled through my brain, still remnants of my own addiction to hope that things could have turned out differently.

In that moment I looked back at his sneakers and wondered what he took with him and if it was worth it. And then I remembered the occasion we went to the movies together to watch *Ghost*, starring Patrick Swayze and Demi Moore. I loved that movie and especially the love and the pain generated by the actors. It was very well done.

Afterwards, walking home, my husband turned to me and asked: "What is it you get to take with you when you die?"

I looked at him and said, "The love inside." He looked back at me with a knowing glance and a sweet smile. This moment, vivid in my memory, now locked within the eternal depth of my soul. I know he got to take the love with him, and nothing else mattered.

Driving away from his house, I had a new awareness and felt grace at work. Not that I was over the grief; it just helped me to find a little peace inside. A peace I clung to as I made my way through the learning curve I was faced with next.

Radical Trust
is not 99%
It is 100%
ALL in.

Chapter Nine

UNDERSTANDING RADICAL TRUST

Trust fall
Everything
All
The death and
The birth

 As executor of the estate, I had to make business decisions I was ill-equipped to understand or handle. I had to take on business partners, pursuing them to redeem what belonged rightfully to my husband and now his family. This included some hard negotiations, in which I had no previous experience.

His business partners insisted his share was less than a fifth of what I sensed it was worth. I had to fight them every step of the way, which proved very hard, not having any facts about his business or its value. Only a knowing inside guided me plus one mention he made a few months earlier, of the value of his partnership with this company.

After a long, gruelling year with financial people, lawyers, and accountants, I won my case, resulting in my receiving a great deal more money. It was an amount I had never imagined having in my whole life. Enough to secure the property in the vision that followed me around.

Along with the money, there surfaced incredible guilt, kind of a double whammy with the pain associated with letting go of my partner and father figure for my daughter. It came with thoughts like *I should have tried harder with him. Perhaps, I could have helped him if I had known more about his illness.* And now I had all this money, but at the cost of this man's life. It took a long time, and a lot of healing work, to understand I bore no blame and it hadn't been part of my plan. It came down to his destiny and God's plan.

At last I had an explanation for why, so mysteriously, I was led back to my marriage after our two-and-a-half-year separation. I had to obey this deep inner call: the radical trust it took to do what I was told to do in spite of absolutely no understanding whatsoever of my actions.

A lawyer pointed out to me, many months later, if I hadn't gone back with my husband for those three months (not one day less would have worked), the insurance company and the courts would have had the right to treat our split as a de facto divorce, since it would have amounted to a four-year separation in total. But because I went back for three months, it cancelled out the nearly three years before going back, leaving less than a year of separation instead. This made me the sole beneficiary of the will.

The consequence of this proved enormous, as this inheritance provided me with more money than I had ever known before and enough to begin a lifelong dream. Some may call it coincidence, but I know it was the workings of a Higher Power and looking back I believe my husband's spirit was involved. This extraordinary development secured an awakening of radical trust within me. Following instructions from a deep place within anchored a new revelation and guidepost for me to access.

Not until a few years later did I fully understand why this money had come to me and how it had been orchestrated from some other reality, and how this obedience to radical trust formed a significant factor in my destiny. To suddenly have things change so dramatically was a huge transition. It seemed like a test I had to pass.

Once I received the money, there was an exigency to invest it as quickly as possible for safekeeping. I didn't trust myself to know how to handle it well, and I still felt the threat that something bad could happen to me because of it. My daughter was devastated from the loss of her dad, and it was one thing I couldn't fix for her, though believe me, I tried. I think the biggest pain for her was how sudden and unexpected his death was, and there was no warning or communication from him. Just the void.

Instinctively, one day I sat down and wrote my little girl a long letter telling her what I wanted her to know should anything happen to me before she became an adult. I was afraid of leaving her an orphan and her not having a communication from me as well. I poured out my heart to her, telling her what I would want her to know as a young girl, teenager and adult. I started the letter by saying "If I am taken from you before you are an adult then it is because you can handle it. God only gives the toughest assignments to the best students."

In the middle, I just let my heart speak to her. I shared stories and intimate soulful messages. I ended the letter with: "It is my hope on your 21st birthday we sit down with a glass of wine and open and read this letter together. Love you and will be with you forever, Mumma."

This letter was locked away with my will and would only be needed in the event of my death before my daughter reached twenty-one. I believe this is something powerful to do for all parents, because you never know when you're called home to spirit, and it prepares your children a little more instead of them having no contact. It could also be done in a video or audio version.

Next, I went about finding a reputable financial advisor. A reference came via a friend, whose husband had already invested over one million dollars with this man.

In a posh downtown office on the twenty-sixth floor, I met Mr. Bill P. Right away he seemed professional, and because I had received a strong referral, I let him lead me down the garden path. More about this later.

What caught my attention was when I shared with him about my vision of a retreat centre, he told me he had been one of the founders of a large spiritual centre in Toronto. However, every time I talked to him about finding land and beginning this retreat, he said it was not a good investment and he could get me a better ROI. He didn't understand it was not a return on my investment I was interested in, but a return on my soul.

Nevertheless, I allowed him to set up my portfolio, most of which I did not understand, but I thought since he spoke spiritual jargon and seemed established, he must be a person I can trust. Right?

It included a $350,000 mortgage investment trust that I totally didn't understand, but he was persuasive and I felt naïve and uninformed about matters of investments. I let him place nearly all the funds (over a million dollars) into investments he said would get a great return.

PART TWO – THE STORY OF XENIA

Chapter Ten

WHEN A VISION HAS YOU

The flow of the river
certain of it's calling
there may be obstacles
but the seed
will become the fruit

A year after this terrible tragedy befell our family, the vision following me around like a loyal dog reared its head again. It was the vision I had at the treehouse, which remained indelibly burnished into my psyche.

It entailed a place, a sanctuary for people to come and share the mystery of nature and silence in a loving, caring and safe environment. It had many acres of land, beautiful rich meadows, gardens, and wildflowers in the vision. I saw abundant trees and creeks, waterfalls, and ferns galore. Of course, it would have horses and other four-legged friends. I received the message it would provide a place for the inner child within all to feel safe to be creative.

It was rousing to stand on the threshold of knowing this could become a reality. This is where I learned you do not have a vision, a vision has you. Relentless in its pursuit for manifestation, it has you completely and utterly.

I managed to free up a few hundred thousand dollars to invest, separate from all the other funds that had already been locked up in other investments. My financial adviser adamantly opposed my seeking land and beginning this vision. He said it would be costly and there would be no ROI. I listened for a while but this rousing feeling wouldn't let up and the curiosity of what could unfold was compelling. Finally I went against his advice and began looking to manifest this vision into reality.

To that end, I found myself a real estate agent on Bowen Island. I knew if I went to the far-out regions of "Fort St. Somewhere," I could buy more acreage, but because I loved Bowen Island so much, I decided to see what I could find. I figured I could afford approximately two or three acres.

I took some time to think about why I had waited so long to go for my vision when I had the money available two years earlier. Why I hesitated and went with the "expert" advice instead of trusting myself.

The real estate agent showed me many different places on Bowen, but nothing felt right. I took my time and had fun playing with the idea of actually doing this. One day, while contemplating this whole idea of a retreat centre, I remembered the original vision and realised it involved not two-to-three acres, but more like forty. It literally had fields and woods. But it was well beyond my budget. I asked myself if I should compromise my vision to stay on the island where my soul felt at home. Should I go off to Northern BC or Timbuktu where I could afford the vision in my head? *Damn, why had I not thought of this sooner, before making those other investments?*

Gail, the realtor, had an instinct that bypassed my desire to purchase only two acres. Somehow, she sensed more closely what I needed, and she got it absolutely right.

One day the phone rang, and it was Gail, all excited. "Angelyn, I have a place I would like to show you. They haven't listed yet." My curiosity was aroused, and we arranged to meet the next day.

As we drove toward the place, Gail said, "I have to tell you I'm taking you somewhere much more than what you've asked for, but it does match the vision you shared with me and I have an intuitive feeling about it for you."

"That's okay, Gail," I assured her. "I'm happy to see it."

Soon, we arrived at a thirty-eight-acre property in the middle of Bowen Island that backed onto Killarney Lake, an area dear to my soul. It was surrounded by hundreds of acres of park and crown lands.

My heart missed a beat as we drove onto the property and I saw fields and trees. My cells tingled with recognition. This was it—this came from the Vision. All at once, it hit me: it had thirty-eight acres and must cost a pretty penny. Gail told me the price, and they were asking at least three times more than I could afford.

"I know it's more than you said, but perhaps you could find investors or partners?" Gail said, attempting to find solutions.

When I first walked on this land, I knew it was sacred and we had a purpose together. The only problem was I didn't have the funds available, but as we drove away that day, I vowed I would find a way.

During the next months I would prowl its meadows and sit with the trees, trying to figure out how I could buy this parcel of land. My cells and heart assured me I would; it would just come down to a matter of how and when.

In the beginning, I sought partners and investors to help buy and restore the land to which I had grown so akin. Without exception, they all saw a broken-down sheep farm and nothing of the magic and beauty I envisaged.

I also tried some of the big banks, sharing my vision with them and asking for a mortgage. They wanted a business plan, to which I replied, "Well, I don't have a business plan, but I do have a vision and a small down payment." They pretty much laughed me out of the bank and sent me on my way.

Although these responses challenged my inner perceptions, the signals and insights persevered.

For the first three months, I remained excited, feeling for sure a perfect solution would reveal itself. But, alas, I could not find one. For certain, I attracted interesting people, curious about investing, but no one related as intimately with the vision as I did. They offered to clear-cut the land and develop it, sell the trees and build a housing estate. The land and buildings had fallen into such a state of ill-repair, it was hard to see through the debris to its potential.

Many times, I would be busy doing something and get this impulse to go over and be on the land. It seemed funny because I had such a strong feeling of connection with this place, as if my bones had been buried there before. I couldn't explain the bond I felt, but a deep knowing insisted on my attention. This place had come in the vision, and I need look no further. The only question was, how?

One day, after walking around the perimeter of the land, I became aware of the magnitude of stewardship I would undertake if I bought it. There must have been hundreds of trees, including one of the oldest Douglas fir trees left on Bowen Island, approximately a thousand years old. The first time I saw it, I wanted to drop to my knees; I felt so humble and small. Yes, thirty-eight acres seemed a lot of land to care for.

My ego asked, "Who do you think you are to create a retreat centre?" Carrying the baggage of doubt around didn't stop me, and I continued to feel optimistic. I considered selling my house but felt it irresponsible to my daughter since the property had no building fit for us to live in.

After a great deal of struggling and incredible sadness, I let it go as a silly idea. In spite of a deep connection to this land, I blocked it out of my mind and heart.

One night I woke from my sleep to a dream about the ancient tree on this land. I dreamt I was inside of this tree and it was full of beautiful amethyst crystals and stairways spiralling upwards. It was like a whole city, and I was aware of myself being very small, almost like an ant or fairy. The tree spoke, telling me it was not finished its work here on Earth and needed me to protect it.

As I went downstairs to make my tea in the morning, this request stayed front and centre in my consciousness for hours. *You mean I'm going to buy this land, if I can, to save this tree?* For days I couldn't get this request out of my mind. Eventually, I let the whole crazy idea go, and other than thoughts and wishes arising in my consciousness, I got on with life without it.

Nearly one full year later, I attended a one-day workshop at the Pan Pacific Hotel in Vancouver with Wayne Dyer and Deepak Chopra. I sat in the front row, my favourite spot, so I could pay attention to everything they said. I found it inspiring, and something Deepak said spoke to me deeply and directly. He said, "*There's something you do that is unique to you, and you do it better than anyone else in the world. If you can find out what that is and do it, you will feel fulfilled.* " It resonated for me, and I pondered it throughout the night.

The next morning, sitting on the boardwalk at Killarney Lake, my favourite contemplation spot, I asked a question to my inner guidance about going back to work. Two years had passed since my husband had died, and I could feel it was time. I felt a desire to do something meaningful in the world and commit to my life's work. So, I closed my eyes and stated my intention: "*How can I be of service?*' For a moment, I mused on the way the words came out. It wasn't the way I would normally pose a question. It was time for me to go back to work, and I was looking for guidance: For example, should I go back into the corporate world or what? But "How can I be of service" was the way it came out.

Immediately, energy rose through my stomach and into my heart and forehead. A message came: *Buy the land behind you and begin the retreat centre.*

"Oh, no," I screamed. "Not that again. I've already let it go. No, give me another assignment." Furiously, I stomped off the boardwalk, giving a glance behind me to the land with which my heart had fallen in love. A little further up the trail I could feel the truth in this request and a peacefulness arising from the depth of my soul.

Over the next couple of days, I pondered this instruction and mused on the possibility of actually being able to pull this off. The feeling at the boardwalk felt so clear and convincing but I still did not know how. Also, I was sure it must have sold in the year since I last visited the idea. One way to find out was to call and at least see if it was still available.

With fingers crossed, I made the call to the realtor and to my great joy, it hadn't sold. I took that as a positive sign and the really good news was the market had softened within the year bringing the price down significantly. In spite of several previous rejections from banks when I shared my vision with them, this time, I found a way to make it happen. I found a wonderful bank manager from Vancity who listened to me and gave me the mortgage when other banks had refused. When the contracts were all signed, I sent an enormous bouquet of flowers to her at her office. She believed in me and she believed in my vision.

In spite of being severely challenged by my financial adviser, who was trying to squeeze out every last investment dollar into another of his schemes, twelve weeks later, I had my name on the title of this beautiful property. It was July 21, 1994 at 4:00 p.m. and I will always remember the moment I signed the real estate purchase agreement.

Later that evening, friends gathered with me around the big tree in a drumming circle, and later we shared a couple of bottles of champagne as we celebrated this miracle back at my house.

The structures on the land were truly dilapidated – there's no other word for it – with every building in major disrepair. The energy felt dense and sad. It would be an enormous project; not for the faint of heart.

And, thank God, I had no idea of the extent of the undertaking at the time. A bit like having a baby. Have you ever noticed how, until you have a child, you cannot imagine such an all-consuming experience? Nobody can ever explain adequately. You have to experience it first-hand. My buying this land felt like that.

We removed over twenty five large green containers of garbage, every part of it, run down. Two redeeming factors were the ancient tree close to the entrance and the oldest dwelling on Bowen Island, though at the time, it looked more like an old shack than a heritage piece.

I had to own the visionary within me to see the potential of this place and, thank God, Chrystalle and I could keep pace with the divine plan unfolding.

Chapter Eleven

WHO DO YOU THINK YOU ARE?

Doubt is the killer
of the flame
Don't let anyone
blow out your candle

 The honeymoon phase lasted approximately three months. Which was perfect because I couldn't take over the place until the sheep-farming cycle was complete, though I could still visit and begin my relationship with the land. I found myself sitting in the fields in blissful awe, contemplating the transformation of these thirty-eight acres. I was able to look beyond the work needed to restore and begin the vision in my head.

Unfortunately, as in most honeymoon phases, it disappeared swiftly, in this case when my dad arrived from England.

Giving him a tour of the property, I felt so excited and proud to show him my new venture. We strolled up the hill toward what was then a junkyard of leftover metals, and I told him about what would happen up there in the future. He seemed a bit agitated as he put his head in his hands and said, "Oh, my God, Angelyn, what have you done? Seriously, I'm worried for you."

At that moment, the vision I'd projected over the old rundown shacks and the land fell down. Collapsed like a screen in a movie set. Suddenly, the mess became all I could see. It was a total nightmare. And all I could think was, *what have I done? Oh, no. What have I done?*

The dilapidated old sheep farm in 1992

Dad returned to England, leaving me panicking. I doubted my vision and myself, invalidating it and saying to myself, like a scolding parent, *What vision? You must have made it up. Wow, what a fraud. Open your eyes. What a mess the place is in. Who did you think you were to pull it off, anyway?*

I knew nothing about renovations, creating a retreat centre, or taking care of hundreds of trees and land. I had very little money left over to create this dream. I knew nothing about business or marketing or anything, for that matter. *Oh, my God, what have I done?* I felt ignorant and beat myself up fiercely. What was I thinking?

In my haste to find out what to do next, I set up a meeting with about twenty experts to come to my house and tell me what to do. It was a Saturday night and I put out some appetizers and drinks and invited them to share their wisdom with me.

This willing group of helpers graciously shared their expertise in marketing, business plans, building, gardening and entrepreneurship. They were kind and happy to give me their best advice. I took notes throughout the evening, and my heart grew heavier and heavier as I imagined all the work I had to do.

Yikes, my mind was telling me I had to do all the marketing, all the renovations, all the bed-making, and all the business, clean up the mess, etc., etc., etc. I thought I had to do it all alone. The more ideas they offered, the deeper into the pit of despair I sank, though, on the outside, I put on my happy face.

After thanking these well-meaning people and seeing them out the door, I collapsed into a deep, dark hole and faced the inevitable: I was a loser and had to sell the land. Who did I think I was? I had such intense doubt! I fell into bed, sick to my stomach, praying I would have answers by the morning.

To no avail. I awoke sad, thinking of ways to get out of this gracefully. After all, I had declared to the Bowen Island community and to my friends and family I would create this amazing, world-class retreat centre. I had a big knot in my stomach and felt humbled by the whole thing.

Then my answer came. At about eleven that morning, I received a phone call from the previous owner of the property. Her husband and mine had died the same year. It surprised me to hear from her, as we didn't have a friendship or know each other. We had met only once, when she shared her husband's dream of having a community on the land. I shared my vision with her, and she had hoped I would be the one to buy the land.

So, here she was calling me.

"Hello, Angelyn, Carol Fernie here. I was just calling to find out how your project is coming along?"

I couldn't hide the grief in my voice. "Well, Carol, I love the land. It's dear to my heart, but I think I've gone in over my head. I feel so overwhelmed and like I've made a big mistake. I don't know what I was thinking, and now I have to sell it."

Calmly, she said, "Angelyn, can I ask you a personal question?"

"Why, yes, of course," I responded.

"Do you believe in a higher intelligence?" she asked.

When she spoke those words, my body released and opened. "Yes, I do." I was in awe of her question.

She said, "Well then, all you have to do is get clear, and everything will be provided and handled."

That was it. I thanked her, and we hung up.

It took me a moment to register what had happened. This guardian angel had called out of the blue, just at this most vital moment. And it brought the awareness I didn't work alone, and I didn't do this by myself. I felt confused, as I'd thought this was all about me doing this, and suddenly I realised it wasn't. Instead, it was about a lot of people: Chrystalle and a huge community would develop with this project and, most importantly, spirit. I was not alone. What a huge relief, and I thank God for her phone call that day. The fear and isolation I felt melted away, and a growing trust began. My instincts had not led me astray, and they gave me the courage to go on.

Many years later, Dad returned and accused me of taking him to a different place. He said, "This isn't the place you took me to before." And then he made a statement that floored me: "Well, Angelyn, if anyone can pull this off, you can." Why hadn't he given me his confidence earlier when I really needed it. All I could do was shake my head and smile.

Chapter Twelve

THREE CLEAR INSTRUCTIONS

The Vision's strong
build it for they will come
When the rain falls
And the forest speaks

 Over the ensuing years, hundreds of thousands of dollars were poured into cleaning up, restoring, and building the retreat centre. Volunteers came to support the project, allowing us to stretch each dollar in ways unimaginable. The land and energy changed radically through the hundreds of people who contributed their love, skills and strength.

Right away, Visions (which is what I called my retreat centre at first) attracted volunteers to help us, and it always amazed me when they would come and work all day and phone to thank me the next day. My dad couldn't get his head around this concept. "You mean people come and sweat and work hard all day and then thank you? What? How? Why?"

I would say, "Yes, Dad, that's what happens here, and it happens all the time. People love to come, be of service, and be part of a creative community, and that's what this place provides."

From the very beginning, this project was soul guided. It seemed as if we had been set up for eons to carry out this enormous task. It has taken unshakeable commitment to the vision, willingness to sit in the void while nothing appeared to be happening, and obedience and persistence to see it through. These qualities I had to develop, and my inspiration came from the story of one of the most famous retreat centres in the world, Findhorn[2] in Scotland. The first time I ever read the books written by the co-founder, Aileen Caddy, I devoured them. *This is my story*, I thought, *oh my God*. I knew it wasn't for Visions Retreat to expand into the size of Findhorn, but the roots were definitely the same.

I travelled to Findhorn to attend a conference on Community and Leadership. It was an inspiring eye-opener. There I met Patch Adams[3] and loved getting to know him and hearing his story. He impacted me because he too had a big vision, which in his case was to create a free hospital for

---

[2] www.findhorn.org
[3] https://www.patchadams.org/patch-adams/

. One night he and I were literally the last ones leaving the local pub as we shared story after story. (It was wonderful watching the movie produced years later about his life. And they sure got the casting right, with Robin Williams playing the role as Patch).

I shared a room with two wonderful ladies, one from Munich, Elinor Kolbeck, and the other from New Zealand, Saranya. At first I didn't want to share a space with anyone, but as luck would have it, I found myself partnered with the perfect roommates for my journey. They both became global soul sisters, and we have met throughout the years in different countries. They visited my retreat centre many times, and Elinor even brought her group from Germany for her program. Now I am an advocate for sharing rooms whenever possible.

A great thing I discovered at Findhorn was the most magical game, The Game of Transformation®.[4]
I highly recommend it, especially if you are looking for insight and inspiration. It was created and developed by Joy Drake and Kathy Tyler at the Findhorn Foundation in the mid-seventies.

---

[4] https://www.findhorn.org/programmes/transformation-game-alchemy/

It is a game where you hold a focus or intention, and though you are playing with others, it truly is your own game. It's also great to have others witnessing your journey and you play with Angels, Insights and Setbacks. The game is played on four levels, physical, emotional, mental and spiritual, and in that order. It can be one or two hours long or go on for several hours and sometimes days.

The symbolism is often stunningly accurate. Many years later, back home, I was playing it with friends when a group miracle happened. I'll explain:

The game is usually for four participants but this particular evening we made it work for five, including myself, my dear friend Arletti, her brother Ken, another soul sister Julie Blue, and Diane. It was getting close to midnight and we were wilting and wanting to finish the game, but we were all stuck on the Spiritual level. I suggested, "I know, how about if we roll the dice and all roll the same number, we will call it done and we can wrap it up." *Good luck* thought the shared ego in the room. Chuckling away at the possibility, the first person threw the dice and got 5. The next person got 4, the next something else and we thought *of course we couldn't all roll the same number; who did we think we were, God?*

Wearily we resumed playing, and one of us got a card that said, Group Setback, which means lowest roller gets this card. The first person rolled a 1 . . . *haha*, we snickered, thinking, *the setback was theirs*. The second person rolled 1; wow, a tie for lowest roller. The third person rolled 1, the fourth person rolled 1 and the fifth rolled 1. We literally screamed and ran outside on the deck where we were greeted with the full moon lighting the sparkling ocean beneath. Indulging in the magic as we danced around on the deck in awe, one of us said, "I wonder what the setback was." We went back in the house and the card read: *You are set back by your doubt on your present level.* (Spiritual).

I will never forget this game; it was profound and gave me the confidence to keep listening and trusting the guidance being given.

FINDING MY RETREAT CENTRE'S NAME

Many unanswered questions remained about the specifics of how to unfold this vision. I stalked all the clues and messages to find my answers. First, I wanted to find out the fitting name for my retreat centre. Visions Retreat didn't feel like the right name.

I attended a songwriter's retreat at Hollyhock on Cortes Island, with Chris Williamson[5]. In one of the sharing circles I made it known I was looking for a name for my retreat centre. After lunch one day, Chris came

---

[5] www.criswilliamson.com

back after visiting the small library upstairs, and she announced she thought she may have the suitable name. It was Xenia, which means hospitality in Ancient Greek. It also signifies "friend of the stranger and cross-pollination of ideas between guest and host." I cannot remember the name of the book she was reading from, but I checked it out later from different Greek references and found it to be suitable. *Wow, how appropriate*, I thought. It felt right and I knew it was correct, so Xenia Creative Development Centre was birthed.

WHAT IS THE THEME OR PURPOSE?

Next, I asked: What is the overall theme? What did the land ask for? What kind of programs should be offered?

Even while groups were coming, I continued asking for clear instruction for three-and-a-half years. What is the premise, the direction? What, specifically, is supposed to go on here? I would pray, ask, demand, and downright beg. However, nothing came. All I got were instructions to "build another bathroom, get the chicken coop cleaned up, build this, do that, etc."

Many times, I used my logic to determine what it *should* be, but I always felt dissatisfied, like a train not sitting properly on its track.

My next strategy, and to appear professional, was to create a business plan. It took a lot of work because there were many aspects I didn't yet know. How to unfold the vision hadn't come clear, and I learned I had to be patient. I filed the business plan away and have not looked at it since.

In the meantime, and from the beginning, we hosted many excellent workshops, with great teachers showing up seemingly out of the blue. Our guests were extremely patient and forgiving as we plumbed in toilets around them. They loved watching the changes each time they returned to Xenia.

My searching for clarity continued on a trip to England.

One day, while visiting a silent retreat centre in the southeast of England, one of the missionaries showed me around. She made tea for me, and we sat in an elegant library and chatted about the future plans for St. Julian's.

The walls were full of mystery and stories from centuries gone by. As we visited the mansion, I particularly loved the chapel, set up like a barn with straw on the floor and simple wooden chairs. A huge diamond window hung behind the altar, bringing in the outdoor foliage and beauty. It registered as something I wanted to add to our sacred spaces as they were being built.

Stepping out into the garden, I felt a need to go off by myself for a while. I stood there basking in the picturesque English garden and surrounding countryside. It was strikingly beautiful and there was a sweet aroma in the air. Cows grazed in the rolling meadows beyond, and I sank into a deep love and oneness with nature.

As I stood there, I became mesmerized with this stillness permeating my entire body. I became one with the landscape. The silence and stillness became all that existed in that moment. I don't know how many minutes passed, but I felt a deep and profound knowing moving through my body and a connection between this place and mine. I tracked clues, but not until a couple of months after, did I receive the full information.

Later that year, I was sitting up in the old sawmill site at Xenia and thought about how and when we would get around to cleaning up the discarded junk and metals dumped there decades earlier. I saw the discarded trucks, fridges, bicycles, stoves, and huge mounds of shavings from the old, now-abandoned sawmill. Somehow, I could see beyond the generations of mess left behind. I sensed something sacred about the place.

The sun felt warm on my face, and joy welled up inside as I sat there on an old stump with my two dogs, contemplating the day. I'm not sure how long I had been sitting there when suddenly, out of the silence, came three distinct messages, as clear as a bell. A total inspiration filled all my senses as I saw what was being asked of me. It was to:

1. **Build a labyrinth, here and now.**
2. **Build a chapel.**
3. **Introduce the work of Silence to all who come.**

All at once, I had complete clarity about what I should do, and it connected directly to that day at St. Julian's in England.

I should offer my retreat centre as a place of connection to the land and awaken people to silence.

What? This took me completely by surprise. It didn't reflect the direction I had imagined. As a community, we had dreamed up so many different ideas as to what it should be. When I recall the original vision, it was to be *"a sanctuary in nature where the child within all can feel safe to be creative."*

I thought this meant we had to produce all kinds of projects and programs to bring forth this creative muse. Maybe an artist colony or even a small residential community. But, instead, the opposite was true; it was just to hold out a container into which the creativity or healing can occur. *We are the holders of the space.* A sense of deep inner peace moved through me once again, and I realised I had arrived at the answer I had quested for so long. I had been trying to complicate something so simple. Now I understood more deeply the partnership Xenia would offer to all groups and individuals staying there.

Upon looking at the mess in front of me, I laughed out loud at the request just made. A major clean-up was in order.

I had little knowledge of labyrinths at the time but remembered a book a friend had given to me a year earlier, called *Walking a Sacred Path,* by Dr. Lauren Artress[6], and for some reason, I hadn't yet read it. Of course, the first thing I did was run and find this book and read it.

Digging into this subject, I soon learned there is a huge interest in this powerful tool, spanning many cultures and traditions dating back some 4,000 years. I enrolled in a five-day facilitator's training with Dr. Artress at Grace Cathedral in San Francisco. Hopefully, it would prepare me for the immense archetypal form I was told would impact many thousands of people's lives. I discovered it is an ancient mystical tool being resurrected and used in a variety of ways in hospitals, schools, and even corporate parking lots for stress management. Dr.

---

[6] https://labyrinthsociety.org/

Artress was a major instigator of this resurrection. I enjoyed working with this sincere, inclusive visionary. She says the labyrinth has three stages: Purgation, Illumination, and Unity.

Purgation is where you purge your mind of chatter and doubt and settle down as you make your way to the centre. The centre is referred to as "Illumination," and in this place you may feel the emptiness or the void. To sit in this quiet, still place is illuminating and spacious. Often, inspiration and ideas greet you on the way out of the centre. Unity unfolds and thoughts flow as to how to take these insights out into the community.

- **<u>The Birth of the Labyrinth</u>**

The moment we said "yes," the miracles unfolded rapidly. People came to help clean up and prepare the container for this mysterious request. In all my life, I had never seen energy move so fast. We had community work parties recycling all the metals and burn piles as we removed sludge and grime from the area. It seemed hard to identify it as a meadow until weeks later when the circle of large trees revealed themselves.

After the meadow was cleared and prepared, it took fifty volunteers four days to create our eleven-circuit, eighty-eight-foot Hopi/Celtic labyrinth.

On the second day me, Chrystalle, our dear soul sister Ellen Hayakawa and her friend Harriot Royer went up to the labyrinth site and something mysterious happened. The day before, we had constructed the first part of the Labyrinth, which was the cross in the centre.

Early that morning, a low-lying fog filled the meadow. Though quiet, we all sensed an energy, and then, to our utmost surprise, we saw something hovering about fifty feet over the stone pathway forming the cross. We grew alarmed and wondered what it was. Chrystalle took out her camera and shot pictures of it. It literally fried her camera, but we still managed to access the photos.

Pretty soon this flying saucer type form lifted up and disappeared. The four of us witnessed this visitation and felt it a blessing, rather than any kind of threat. I'm so glad the four of witnessed this together. There were many symbols in the visitation and we each saw unique images. It felt like we were being observed, and I think we checked out fine given our guidance and sincerity.

The two-thousand-plus stones gathered from the land became the Labyrinth's pathways. It was a wonder-filled and inspiring process. The Labyrinth opened officially on September 17, 1997, in a joyful candlelight celebration.

In the more than two decades since then, many hundreds (maybe even thousands) of labyrinths have sprung up all over the world.

One day, years later, I was up in the Labyrinth, sitting on a stone in the centre, when I heard the message: "Are you the keeper of the Labyrinth?"

I looked around to see if this message could be for anyone else. Again, I heard it: "Are you the keeper of the Labyrinth?"

Since there was nobody else present, I assumed it must be me. "Yes. Yes, I am the keeper of the Labyrinth," I replied, finally.

"Good, then why has the sawdust sat in a pile outside the Labyrinth for so long? When will you finish the job?"

Aghast, I looked at the sawdust pile brought there during the youth mentoring program the previous summer. The task never got completed. For some reason, it had become part of the scenery and forgotten.

With a jolt, I ran out of the centre of the labyrinth and headed down to the tool shed to fetch a wheelbarrow and shovel. I could have rounded up a team to help me, but I wanted to do this alone. It took quite some effort, but it also provided time to be in the moment with the Labyrinth and in service to it. Soon, I had completed the work and felt grateful for the "gentle reminder."

I reflected on being called the Keeper of the Labyrinth and what this, in fact, meant. Obviously, because I had received the original message to build the Labyrinth, I must also have agreed to become the keeper. I realised what a responsibility and privilege this was.

• The Chapel

The Chapel, which today we refer to as the Sanctuary, happened next. When I tuned in to where it should be located, I saw it would occupy the same spot where Tarla, one of our community members, was building a small cabin for himself.

Oh, no, it can't be that spot! I thought, *Tarla will get upset, turning his plan into the Chapel.* I dismissed the location idea right away because I didn't want to confront him. He worked as the fire keeper of the sweat lodge we'd had on a regular basis, and I'd given him permission to build on the property. How could I change my mind?

Unfortunately, this was not a nebulous or fanciful idea but instead, an assignment. And I had received the instructions. So, the day came when I told Tarla the message I had received about where this chapel was to be built. In fact, I told him, he had started building it already.

It took a lot of courage for me to tell him this information, and I had to deal with the doubt inside my head asking if I *really* got these instructions or if I made them up. I felt terrible about asking him to change plans, but I knew the importance of listening, even if not one other person understood. I would not have managed to steward this land and mission if I had stopped because of what other people thought. I had to remain willing to become absolutely alone and committed in order to follow direction. Sometimes, it is a lonely path to have to be the one to make difficult decisions about things like this and even to disappoint others in the process. It didn't feel easy but, gently, I asked Tarla to remove the loft and leave the high ceiling because it wouldn't be a building to sleep in but a place for people to meditate. As you can imagine, he didn't feel so happy at first but, to his credit, got on board relatively quickly.

Tarla Curran and Matthew Smith spent their weekends building the Chapel. They made it with such love, you can feel it in the walls. An eternal candle holds vigil twenty-four hours a day during our silent retreats, and it stands on a table in front of a large diamond window inspired from St. Julian's barn Sanctuary in England.
The silence in this space feels extraordinary and easier to access. The Chapel is a
vortex, a divine intervention, through which internal

chatter 'shuts up' and gets ordered down like an obedient dog.

I realised the power and significance of this Chapel and why it needed to be built. For me, it represents a culmination of experiences I have had with silence, and I marvel at the synchronistic value placed in our hands.

In the opening ceremony, Tarla handed the finished Sanctuary over to Xenia officially for the purpose indicated, and declared it was completely unconditional. In the end, he admitted he too felt the truth in the vision given. Tarla and Matthew even said they started calling it the Sanctuary before they knew it was to become one.

• **The Work of Silence**

The third instruction of introducing silence took four years to begin and, finally, in 2002, we offered the first Vigil Silent Retreat, which has proven a unique and powerful process to bring about the silence and listening. The Labyrinth, Nature, and the Sanctuary act as bridges into the silence, and I understand now why the three messages came all at the same time.

So that was our blueprint for Xenia. Three instructions, which were to serve as an umbrella under which many variables could sit. In the course of unfolding this master plan, we did veer off-course before we got it right, creating much confusion and struggle. Many times we wanted to give up, but something inside encouraged us to "just keep going."

Our programs were and are still profound and people were being helped in ways I had not imagined. If you read from our earliest Guest Books you will see the theme weaving through all of their comments. *Xenia is magical; I felt so at home; I felt safe enough to truly explore the truth of my pain; My creativity soared while I was at Xenia; There's something about this place I cannot explain; My soul feels invigorated here.* One guest who came back many times to volunteer in the garden wrote this:

I thought this miraculous, spiritual experience was in the land—and it is. But I have walked many lands, in India, Africa, Europe, Canada, and the U.S., and have not experienced it before. And then I thought it must come from the structures and holy places like the ancient tree and the Sanctuary—and it does. But I have been in many structures and holy places around the world and have not felt this before. And then I thought it must come from the spirituality of the people there, those dedicated, that enliven the Creative Force—and it does. But I have been with many people in many structures in many lands and have never experienced this kind of spirituality before.'

–Joan O'Flynn

It was clear from the very beginning and confirmed many times since, Xenia was sitting on powerful land and had a divine purpose.

Chapter Thirteen

TREE THAT WALKS

*You look
and wonder the key
It is so simple
it is Love*

 Nestled between the Labyrinth and the Sanctuary is an ancient Douglas fir tree. Somehow, the giant tree avoided the clear-cutting on the island. Its wounds partially sealed with healing bark, stands as a spiritual icon at the gateway of the property. It is a true survivor, scarred by saws and marked by the logger's axe. What a privilege for us to have the presence of this magnificent sentient being grace this land. Early on I asked this  impressive tree, "What is your name?" I heard: *"OPA,"* which I understood to be German for Grandpa. It is also a Greek word and used as an acclaim or celebration, often involving plate-throwing as people shouted "OPA!"

I got the acronym right away: OPA: *Opening Pathways of Awareness,* which would become the subtle basis of our work at Xenia. I giggled to myself at the clarity of the name, and as I was stepping down from leaning against OPA, I heard the whisper: "*And your name is: Tree That Walks.*"

Sweet, OPA tree gave me a name. It would take a few years before I fully understood the acclaim bestowed upon me.

On one full moon, I received a summons out into the night. I felt compelled to stay with OPA for over an hour. The moon shone full, and I had never witnessed such brightness in the night. Aware of my extremely tired body when I arrived at OPA, I simply leaned back into the tree and started relaxing right away. Within half an hour, my whole body became totally energized, and I could have run a marathon. A transmission of some kind had taken place, and I asked how it happened. Here's a short conversation I had with OPA:

Angelyn: *OPA, you are ancient.*

OPA: *You are eternal.*

Angelyn: *You are a healer.*

OPA: *Healing happens when we connect.*

Angelyn: *You have witnessed me, and I have changed.*

OPA: *That you have witnessed me, we have changed.*

Angelyn: *You are sacred.*

OPA: *We are the same.*

Now if ever I am tired, I remember to go and hang out with OPA by simply leaning back and relaxing. Some people liken it to running a defragmentation on your computer. OPA gives love and energy so abundantly.

The Labyrinth, OPA, the Sanctuary, and the stillness are offered freely to the public any time, and people come from far and wide to visit. OPA was also written up in the *Province* newspaper as one of the ten most beloved trees in British Columbia. OPA seems to break the spiritual reserve of visitors. And when you google OPA tree, you will be directed to our OPA at Xenia.

On a visit he made to Xenia, legendary eco-forester Merv Wilkinson estimated this magnificent tree to be between 900 and 1100 years old. So we have settled on a thousand years old. It was a real privilege to host this elderly couple, Merv and his wife Ann. I couldn't get enough of his stories as he made his acquaintance with OPA. It was great to glean wisdom from this environmental hero. They owned and developed Wildwood, a renowned seventy-seven-acre ecoforest on Vancouver Island.

Merv was the proud recipient of the Order of BC, Order of Canada and an Honorary Doctor of Law from the University of Victoria. A true pioneer throughout his life.

9/11

If you're old enough, I'm sure you know where you were on September 11, 2001. I remember it vividly. That day we had a Lakota elder visiting us at Xenia, Wallace Black Elk. He and a crew were recording a documentary of his life. When he arrived on the 10th, he looked like he was about to die. Two people supported him, one on each side as he walked around the place. I thought for sure he had very little time left on this plane.

The next morning, I was awoken, as many of you were, with a frenzy as I tried to make sense of phone calls coming my way. People said, "Turn on the TV!!" Since I didn't have cable, I used a rabbit-ear antenna to tune in and then I saw it. The twin towers were coming down. OMG. The world watched in disbelief.

Wallace had gone down to the local coffee shop with his entourage and came flying back after hearing the news. He gathered us up and took us over to OPA, saying: "This isn't what you think it is. The most important thing I can say is: Keep your hearts open and stay out of fear."

He mentioned he needed to leave right away and get back to his people in Colorado. I told him the border was closed and all flights had been stopped. It was eerie not to hear any airplanes for a day or two. He assured us he would be able to cross the border based on his status, and off he went.

The man that arrived looking like he was about to die was suddenly transformed. He looked twenty years younger, now physically able to walk by himself. It's amazing what can happen when a person feels a strong sense of purpose.; It can even override major physical ailments. He left Xenia on track and on purpose. Within an hour and a half, we heard news that he had indeed cleared the border.

Wallace Black Elk a traditional Lakota Elder and

spiritual interpreter, was a Channupa (sacred pipe) bearing descendent of the legendary Nicholas Black Elk whose visionary experiences were recounted in the book *Black Elk Speaks*.

Wallace Black Elk born in 1921, lived on for a further three years and, I'm sure finished his documentary. He died in 2004.

Photo taken by Angelyn on September 11, 2001

> *"I was stuck in this abiding darkness until the stress became too heavy to bear and finally, I gave myself to the terror in absolute surrender."*

Chapter Fourteen

DARK NIGHT OF THE SOUL

Fear is an illusion
of the mind
watch it and it
disappears

 For the first five years, Chrystalle lived at Xenia and I lived on the other side of Bowen Island in the house I bought with Ron years before. I didn't ever expect to live at Xenia, especially since I already had a home. One day I was working in the Xenia garden doing some weeding when I got this message: *you need to be at Xenia.* I thought, *what do you mean? I am always at Xenia, every day.* The message came: *you need to be here at night with the owls.* I had a sinking feeling in my gut when I considered what this message implied. Where at Xenia would I live with my daughter?

There was only the little cabin up on the hill with a small loft bedroom. I wanted to resist, but I knew it was pointless to object when it came to guidance.

As our carpenter was finishing up his last job that morning, he said, "Angelyn, I'm going to miss you guys and Xenia." He had been working with us for nearly a year with renovations, and today would be his last day. I went over to him and said he actually could stay because now we were going to renovate the cabin so my daughter and I could move to Xenia.

He asked, "What do you mean?" I said I just received a message that I needed to move to Xenia and the cabin was the only place possible for us to move into. He said, "Well, don't you have to think about it first?" He had watched me in the garden weeding and saw I was thinking about something deeply but wasn't sure what.

I said, "No, it wasn't an idea, it was an instruction." I had already been initiated into an inviolable commitment to God's plan.

It was quite the sacrifice to give up this beautiful 3,000 sq.ft. house with panoramic ocean view and move into a little cabin in the woods. It was a radical downsize but one we would have to make.

Unfortunately, it turned out to be a big undertaking once we investigated the foundation, or more accurately, lack thereof. Our $50,000 budget turned into a $180,000 renovation. The roof was taken off and the beams were hoisted into the air while a new foundation was poured.

After several months, it was ready for us to move in to. The renovation was beautiful, and we doubled the size of the cabin, giving my daughter her own bedroom and a treehouse office for me. It became the happiest place I have ever lived. It was no longer referred to as the cabin but instead as Angelyn's enchanted log home.

For the previous five years, I had felt totally in the flow of money, continuing to write cheques as needed. At the back of my mind, though, I had some awareness of how the money was pouring out and much less was coming in. But the spending momentum was so strong, I pushed away the warning signs.

August 11, 1999, marked a moment in time when I knew everything was about to change, and not in a good way. It became the beginning of a descent that would last a few years.

Over a number of months, I felt the restriction of incredible over-expenditure on the Xenia project. I was living an illusion my money source was coming from a bottomless well, and the banks enabled this misperception at first by continuing to gladly loan me more and more money. On top of the Xenia project, my home budget renovation more than tripled. Coupled with this was my lack of focus on the actual business. We were so fixated on cleaning up and renovating, we ignored the important aspects of the overall mission. We had offered a few of our silent retreats but mostly people were coming to facilitate their own programs. Xenia attracted groups into its treasured container before we were officially open.

But people insisted, and we agreed as long as they knew the circumstances. We were also offering programs at prices that didn't cover costs and letting people stay for free. I was caught in the idea of Xenia being a spiritual retreat and I shouldn't charge for that.

Although people were coming and great programs were happening, behind the scenes we were not at all organized and had a lot to learn about running a business.

When I looked at how Chrystalle and I had operated the business, I winced when I came face-to-face with our business naiveté. We were going through a pile of papers in the office one day and discovered over twenty old requests for silent retreats that had not been responded to. Here I thought we'd had little interest, and all the while we had letters, emails, and phone calls from people wanting to register if only they could find out how. It woke me up out of my delusion, and I felt great shame and guilt for such negligence. I thought I had delegated the job, but it wasn't clear, and for that I had to take responsibility.

And an even bigger crisis was brewing. After spending eleven years and hundreds of thousands of dollars transforming the old infrastructure, I suffered severe financial loss from other investments, putting my beloved vision in jeopardy. One day I woke up and found myself in a big dark hole of debt.

This was due to what turned out to be a fraudulent $350,000 mortgage investment trust, finally exposed, and it precipitated a downward domino effect. The financial adviser I had used and trusted turned out to be another Bernie Madoff. He took off to Panama with 3.5 million dollars of investors' money, including $350,000 of mine. As a result, I fell five months behind in the mortgage, three years behind in property taxes, I was receiving disconnection notices, and for the life of me I couldn't find the money to make ends meet and stop the downward spiral.

This whole process took about two years, and I was living in fear every day, which amped up to three months of sheer terror when I learned my beloved Xenia was going into the newspaper for a tax sale. Somehow, I knew this terror was bigger than just losing a property; it was like losing a child. How could I lose Xenia, especially when it was doing incredible work, including programs that empowered street kids and helped to heal adults through a plethora of challenges? It was providing transformation for people who came and found healing and solace.

Week by week, it became increasingly difficult, until I got to the point where we had absolutely no cash flow available, not even to meet the bills, and I hadn't bargained for all the other cash-flow shortages;

investment fraud; other investments that were supposed to be liquid and were not, and the house that was supposed to sell didn't.

Unable to climb above the relentless, spiralling stories back into hope and optimism, my ego had me in its grip and I believed the lies it told me. It said I would lose Xenia and I would die. Of course, the ego always wants to take things to the extreme. Hitting bottom, I had sustained terror in my body for three months. I went to bed in terror and woke up in terror. Never before had I received so many calls from angry debt collectors or so many disconnection notices. I had fallen into a deep dark hole, which impeded my ability to think about solutions.

To the outside world, I looked rich, being a landowner, driving a nice car, having horses and a lovely home. However, it was even harder holding up a big infrastructure I had created when I did not have the money to maintain it. It looked like I was living the dream, but I couldn't actually afford it. I had overextended myself beyond belief. I guess it was a privilege to have a vision and the resources to get it started. The next part would test me in ways I needed in order to fulfil a much bigger vision.

Panicked about losing Xenia and losing everything, I became unbearably hard on myself about the decisions I had made in the past and told myself I must be stupid;

that if I had been better equipped and smart enough, I could have made this work out, and I should let someone more skilled take over. I felt sad and sick to the pit of my stomach. Throughout this period, I was sleeping as much as I could to curtail the pain. I had triggered a financial haemorrhage and now I needed to grow up and learn how to run my business. But I couldn't face it.

As the bills piled in, I didn't even open the envelopes because I knew I couldn't pay them, so what was the point? For months, I had cried myself to sleep and the fear created crippling stress in my body.

One day, while sitting on the floor in my living room with boxes of papers and bills, there was a knock at my door, and I saw my friend Ellen peering in through the glass panel. I motioned for her to come in, not being able to even get up off the floor to greet her. She asked me what was up, and I said, "I can't go on. I've reached the end of my rope. I can't hold on to Xenia anymore. It's over." I showed her my bills and all the reasons why it was over. The vulnerability was extreme, but it was all I had in the end.

Ellen, a rather commanding woman, said, "Get up, Angelyn, you can't give up on your vision. Eileen Caddy never gave up on her vision of Findhorn." She knew that would get me up off the floor and she called it true.

I had discovered Findhorn's origins were so similar to that of Xenia. They didn't have the finances to pull off some amazing miracles but because of their faith and following guidance, Findhorn expanded to become a world-class centre, including thousands of residents and thousands more guests every year. Eileen Caddy had radical trust.

This was the reminder I needed. I managed to get up off the floor and Ellen, firm but lovingly, eased me through the next few hours. Ellen is a person who lives according to spirit and is doing some big work in the world with gifted children and bringing spirit into business. I trusted her and felt like I could believe in her when she said, "Get up; you have to go on." I think this truly precipitated the beginning of my cracking open.

Awareness was prying lose, yet I continued to run from the terror, begging people to help me, trying to sell things, but to no avail. My best friend was cleaning houses and giving me money for food, and my daughter was baby-sitting to help out. I hated that I put my daughter through this ordeal, but it was hard to disguise my terror. One morning I walked my daughter up to the school bus and returned quickly crashing back onto the couch, laying there comatose for hours.

I was stuck in this abiding darkness until the stress became too heavy to bear and finally, I gave myself to the terror in absolute surrender. It was like fire consuming me totally and completely until there was nothing left. No more fear, no more bag lady stories, no more Xenia, no more body. It didn't matter anymore. There was just quiet stillness.

Silence permeated this space, and peace expanded into all I could know in that moment.

It felt like the day after an intense thunderstorm — the earth growing moist from the rain and the air clear. Every muscle relaxed, and a smile arose from a place deep within.

The fire had consumed all the fear and gobbled up the stories, the terror, and even me. A calmness prevailed . . . there were no more problems . . . what on Earth had happened?

Only hours earlier, it seemed as if my whole life had come to an end. At the very least, my dream, my retreat centre, my life, had ended in despair.

How could this all have fallen away? No solution to this problem had presented itself. Yet a peacefulness reigned, and I knew all would turn out okay, no matter what it looked like. I had no more concern. I had met the terror head on. The fire of fear had blown out. It felt like a death.

I knew this would become one of the most significant times of my life and I would learn so much from this dark night of the soul experience, and indeed, this proved true. My perspective had shifted profoundly through this experience. Instead of thinking and worrying my way out of financial problems, I followed instructions from a deep pool of listening inside. This informed me, specifically, to ask for help from some people I knew.

The next day, my friend Ariel and I got on the phone and raised $20,000 of gifted money in three-and-a-half hours. It was such a shift in reality, with an ease and grace I would start to become accustomed to. Ariel's undying faith in me and Xenia had been a pillar of strength I had leaned on and appreciated so much.

I know the people who gave the donations did not have a surplus of money, but they believed in me and wanted to save Xenia from going back to the bank. Ariel certainly didn't have money to give me, but she found a way when I couldn't. Community members helped out as well, and when they gave me this money, they knew it was gifted and they were not expecting it back. Many others joined in, including people I barely knew. We marched down to the bank and put the mortgage back on track and have not faulted on our mortgage payment ever since.

Next another wonderful benefactor showed up and gave us a huge financial gift, which totally cleared off back taxes and we were able to build a couple of new structures.

It's remarkable how different our results are when we come from a place of love and surrender compared to a place of neediness and pleading from our wounded self. For months I had begged for help from every source imaginable. Through all this I learned that coming from an open wound has a repelling energy. Nobody wanted to invest in a sinking ship. The moment I surrendered and handed it over, I got squarely back on my own team; a team that included spirit and radical trust. I lived in a state of love and peace, even though the same conditions remained at first. I knew there was a hemorrhage going on, but I was ready to grow up and learn how to run my business. I became worthy of people's trust and support, attracting what I needed.

I learned you cannot solve money problems with money alone. As I surrendered and trusted in a higher power that desperately wanted to serve through me, I witnessed many miracles unfolding. A contract would come in the day before the mortgage payment fell due. Another time, Chrystalle and I were on the ferry making our way to put out a Home Depot payment fire when we ran into an acquaintance who had just dropped off some items he had donated to Xenia. I was just thanking him for his contribution when he asked me how much money

I needed. I couldn't believe he'd asked me that question because he didn't know anything about our financial problems; but there again, I was probably naïve in assuming that. Likely, it had become way more obvious than I was aware of. He literally asked how much I needed that day. I told him, and he said, "Okay, come down to my truck, and I'll write you a cheque." What? Ridiculous!! Of course, I graciously accepted the gift.

One morning I woke up and could really see all the beauty we had put into the restoration of the physical space and the purity of energy permeating the thirty-eight acres of land; this was truly valuable and reminded me of our competence and creativity. The critical self-talk trying to diminish me had stopped, and I could appreciate a new viewpoint.

Fear was no longer a visitor and if it did stop by, I would simply greet it with my full attention, at which point it gently dissolved.

I did notice a year or so later I had some residual angst associated with the whole thing. Even though I had accepted the situation and had fully surrendered into the fire of fear and came through the other side there was a lingering self-blame about my ignorance in losing a huge amount of money. It was a niggling story still rattling around in my head about having signed the investment contract for $350,000 when something in me had said,

"NO. DON'T SIGN IT." I hadn't listened. In spite of the red flashing lights, I succumbed to the pressure of my adviser and signed it anyway.

Ever since then my mind ran a continuous story: *You shouldn't have signed that document. Why didn't you listen?* And losing this money came down to my poor judgment. One morning, I waited in the ferry line on my way to another lawyers' meeting. I was in the process of suing a bank manager who was found to be in cahoots with the financial adviser, and they were attempting to get me to settle. The stress of working with lawyers and sorting this mess out felt awful, and I wanted to get free of the whole thing. I knew I was a victim of a fraudulent investment, but I felt responsible for my part in being attracted it in the first place.

Sitting in my car in the ferry line-up, I phoned my friend Wendy to catch up. She was well aware of my financial predicament and I was telling her how hard I was on myself for having signed the contract when I shouldn't have. She said not to go on the ferry. She told me to go home instead and she would send me some questions I needed to answer. She said I would find peace from it.

I went home, and Wendy introduced me to the work of Byron Katie. My friend asked me the following questions:
W: So, you shouldn't have signed the paper, is that true?

A: No, I shouldn't have; I had a bad feeling about it.

W: Can you absolutely know for sure you shouldn't have signed it when you did?

A: Well, I still think I shouldn't have. It was a big mistake.

W: Did you sign it?

A: Yes, I did.

W: Then, you were supposed to.

W: How do you react every time you tell yourself the story of how you shouldn't have signed it when you did?

A: I berate myself. I tell myself I'm stupid. I'm mad at myself. I cannot forgive myself for not listening to my instinct screaming NO. I was an idiot to get scammed.

W: Who would you be if you could never believe that thought again, 'you shouldn't have signed the document when you did?'

After a pause, I could feel the tension releasing from my body as I realised the truth of the situation.

A: I would be free. I could see it did happen, and I could do nothing about it now. It was done, and that was that. I was filled with acceptance of what happened. I forgave myself in that moment and haven't looked back.

I realised what happened actually brought many gifts, and it led me to the great work of Byron Katie and much more transformation. It was a $350,000 lesson, and I would not let it affect me one more minute. Struggling with reality was insane, and I had now become sane.

I later attended a nine-day school for the Work of Byron Katie in California. It was life-changing, and it's ridiculous how simple yet potent the four questions and turnarounds are. I highly recommend you check it out. It is a tool now firmly in my toolbox.

I continued to discover deeper and deeper principles through which to live and run my business. In many cases I was appearing to change my mind so much when in fact I was sourcing better ways of doing things and shifting course quicker than my community was willing to go. I could feel the discord as I struggled to figure things out, and it bothered me because I still had remnants from my past addiction of needing to please everyone.

One day I sat at my computer and connected with my angels as I had done years before at the treehouse. This is what came:

Dear Angels,

I feel so guilty about all the people who have helped me and how I commit and then change my mind. This is part of the source of my guilt. Please help to shed light on this and help me understand it.

There is pain from walking the sovereign journey, and everyone who comes to the banquet, or in your case, potluck, brings their dish and themselves to the table. You have to know there is a synchronistic coming and going of all those who choose not to continue forth and know you have a role that is prone to projection. If you cannot let it fall off you like water off a duck's back, then there is something in it for you to look at. When you can state your truth and know in each changing moment you are present, the best and most honest part of you will emerge. As such you can relax and release any guilt.

There is nobody who has come to the table by being dragged there, and it is for them to look at what they feel victimized by. You are not guilty, you never were guilty, and it is only a feeling that blocks your power.

There is a relinquishing of the full reigns and a joining of a team of draft horses, as it were, to join with you and propel xenia to its next heights. Some will feel afraid of this and project their disturbances upon you, but you must hear this soundly — you are not responsible for what is to unfold here. Hold your head high and go with the truth. Some people would like it to remain a small community while others suffer from seeing what it could be with the right management team in place. There is an offer forthcoming and it may feel a little scary, but know this alignment is from the cosmos, not from your programming. It is happening at the speed of light because of its alignment. In fact, it has been aligning for eons and it is just now you can see it. Hold firm on your willingness to be open and watch how you will try to fix it and save everyone in the process. Pay special attention to how your programming can get in your way. You are not responsible for taking care of everyone's needs, but you are responsible for following the divine plan that you have already agreed upon. There will be room for all who are able to move to the next frequency. Those who have done their work can continue. those in denial will drop away — let them. You have travelled down this path before and you know the way.

Trust in the divine alignment and watch for the signs of spring when all at xenia has changed. Changed for the highest and greatest achievement and completion of your primary physical role here. Yes, you have already guessed it clearly — your work is in the world and we need you in other ways. So, learn this lesson and learn it well. Watch out for projections and do not sell out your plan or the divine plan.

And so it is.

Wow, this felt arousing and a little scary. Did this mean I was leaving Xenia? The thought of leaving created a deep contraction in my solar plexus, and I wondered what God had in store for me next. I tried to push it out of my mind as I continued on with the pursuit of finding ways to sustain my retreat centre.

The next two miracles showed up by way of a business opportunity and a cutting-edge transformational tool.

Chapter Fifteen

VEHICLES OF TRANSFORMATION

Hard to penetrate
if you go straight
merge into it
like rain drops in the stream

 My team of draft horses showed up with two very significant plans, and the one could not succeed without the other. This is where I learned that when you are given a vision, you are always given the resources to make it happen, but it may not be obvious in the beginning. You will need courage to carry it out, and some serious work will be called for.

The first vehicle that shifted my reality was<u>:</u>

1/ Instinx[7] It is said, when the student is ready, the teacher appears, and this is when I met Elinor Meney, who is a Peak Performance Coach for Instinx and licensed teacher of other coaches. We connected when I was on that trip to Australia, which is where she was living at the time. After

---

[7] Elinor Meney www.instinx.com

that, she became important in my path of transformation as my coach.

Elinor, born in British Columbia, had moved to Australia with her husband when her two daughters were quite young. Shortly after I met her, she decided to return to BC to be close to her aging parents.

In 2017 Elinor joined the residential Xenia community and together we are offering our global programs.

The process Elinor works with is not a quick-fix tool—though it can be. It's intricate and sophisticated, accurate and permanent, yet so subtle you hardly recognize its effects at first. Glimpses happen along the way, but where you truly see it is upon reflection in a results review, one, two, or three years later. Then you discover you have become a completely different person.

When you look back and compare a situation from before and see how you handled it then compared to now, you will find massive changes. Changes so big as to make a chasm of difference, yet you got nudged along with such baby steps you barely noticed it. The integration happens instantaneously once the shift has occurred.

It builds a person's capacity to handle life better with all its twists and turns and successes and challenges. I have become deeply transformed from working with this tool over many years. I love using it because I never have to get stuck and can work with it myself, thanks to Elinor's passion to teach it. I do believe it is a tool for success on every level and one of self-actualization. I can declare that if I had not found Instinx, my retreat centre would have gone back to the bank. And I would not have been able to honour and excel in the second vehicle of transformation:

2/ Relationship Marketing business: Univera[8]

Through the work I did with Elinor, my perspectives were changing and my capacity to handle my business was expanding. This led me to a business opportunity in the form of relationship marketing, or as it's often referred to, network marketing. This would become the next major vehicle for transformation.

Highly sceptical of this approach to doing business, I had a lot of pre-conceived ideas seemingly justified from a previous brush with the sector some thirteen years earlier.

I held old-paradigm beliefs of what I thought it was and vowed I would never be foolish enough to get sucked into it again. So, when it reared its head, I said "No" with absolute certainty.

---

[8] Univera.com/1162699

Thinking the idea was totally dismissed, I continued on with my quest to find financial resources enough to keep my retreat centre buoyant from one month to the next. After all, I had gotten over the fear of not having enough money and never worried about where it would come from. Somehow, it always came, and often at the last minute, but it did come, sometimes minutes before payments were due, by an unexpected contract. This inner security that the money would come felt okay, good, in fact, but it had its shortcomings, and I was on to it. This living month-to-month with barely ever anything left over seemed too limited. Meanwhile, all the buildings begged for attention, and the costs involved with living in the rainforest on the west coast of Canada ran high.

Then one day I woke up, and one more contract didn't seem to do it for me any longer—in fact, I found myself dreading one more contract or one more person arriving at the centre.

I felt sick and tired of making ends meet and found myself asking for a new way; in short, a miracle. I wanted to find a way to sustain my retreat centre that took the pressure off having to sell more beds. I was done with that game. It was far too much work. Instead, I wanted my freedom, and I wanted to help others in a more meaningful way.

At the time, I led workshops around the process of transformation, and while the workshops were dynamic and useful, when they finished, I never saw those people again. I never knew if their lives had changed from our time together unless they wrote to me, which they often did, but still, I wondered what happened to them afterward. We'd always say we would stay in touch at the end of the program as we hugged each other and felt a slight ripping away of the quick but strong bond created. But too often, we'd never see each other again. Deep inside, I wanted a better way. A sustainable way. At the time, I had no idea how.

As a child I won a jackpot on the slot machines at my dad's British Legion (probably highly illegal but the adults had turned a blind eye). Jackpots had become a bit of a theme throughout my life, but this time I couldn't wait for jackpots anymore, and the feast-and-famine model didn't work. I dreamed big and wanted a monthly consistent jackpot.

So, when the answer to this prayer arrived, disguised as relationship marketing, I dismissed it immediately. No way could this be my miracle. No way. Never. I rejected the person who'd offered this "opportunity" to me. In fact, she called six times in ten days to come and check it out, to which I always replied, "Absolutely not, no way!"

Renee Beth, my friend from Portland, had always impressed me in our earlier conversations about bringing leaders from around the world together to change the way we did education, business, and healthcare. So, it seemed a bit off-track for her to try to recruit me into network marketing.

I had all kinds of judgments about why she would do such a thing; after all, she was a schoolteacher and an executive coach and more than qualified to do professional work. Renee Beth tried every angle to help me see what she could see. I did notice, how extremely committed to this thing she was, like a dog with a bone. After all, she'd driven over 500 kilometres to give me this "gift," as she put it.

Now, what she didn't know was two months earlier, I'd injured my knee. I remember standing in the river after the fall, where I had jumped across from one big rock to another and slipped, scraping the front of my leg and twisting my knee. I stood there for fifteen minutes or so, letting the water wash over the injury while I contemplated how I was going to get home. Then, as clear as a bell, I heard the message:

There's a purpose for this.

Slightly annoyed, I queried, "What kind of purpose?"

You'll see, came the answer.

Renee Beth didn't know I'd injured my leg, but it seemed she was happy when she found out. She gave me "a gift" saying, *it would help me.*

My leg, though not broken, was severely sprained, and I couldn't ride my horse or walk around the lake, which I loved to do every day. So, happily, I agreed to take her products and give her feedback in three days.

She went on to tell me about the company, but her words became gobbledygook as I watched her excitement and animation play out. I knew where she was going, but no way would I go with her. Out of politeness, I said I would take her products, but that's all.

"Angelyn, this is the dream you and I have had for years; to bring leaders from around the world together to build learning communities and help raise the consciousness of the planet. Don't you remember when we sat out on your porch with a glass of wine that day?" she said.

I did but simply couldn't get myself fired up to hear what she had to say. In fact, as I sat in front of her, not listening to a word she uttered, I felt sorry for her. The inner critic came out in full force.

To my surprise, three days later, heading out to the barn to feed the horses, I noticed something felt different. I couldn't feel the pain in my leg anymore. *Wow, I* thought, *this is interesting. Could this be the product Renee Beth gave me?*

I ran back home, thrilled at feeling better, and phoned her. "Renee Beth," I said, "can you please send me more of those products you left with me? I think they helped my leg."

She said she would be delighted to get the products to me, but first I would have to come to Portland to meet her team. In other words, she'd driven all the way to Bowen Island to bring this to me, and now it seemed only fair for me to return the favour and go to her neck of the woods.

I corrected her. "No, no, you misunderstood me. I only want to buy the products. I'm not the slightest bit interested in the business."

She continued to try and light a spark in me but I kept repeating it was not for me. This didn't seem to faze her, either she didn't hear me or she was the most tenacious person I had ever met. I found it to be the latter.

Then, on Sunday evening, she phoned again. My body tensed up when I saw her number on my screen. I nearly didn't pick up the phone, but I felt sorry for her.

"Angelyn, before you say your final no, would you please download the audio clip I just sent you and listen to it. Please, will you do this for me? I'll never bother you again, I promise,' she said.

My body let out a big sigh, and I agreed. It took twenty minutes to download the file, then I reluctantly listened to what Renee Beth was so excited to share with me.

Within five minutes of listening to this rather inspiring interview with a brilliant scientist and a top income earner in this company, something inside me opened up. He spoke of how a billionaire philanthropist, a Wall Street icon CEO, and he had agreed to do their highest and best. They placed their hands on top of each other as a gesture of commitment.

Those three words got my attention—*highest and best.* Hearing this sparked a curiosity of truth. I had not yet achieved my highest and best, but in that moment, I knew I wanted to.

Yes, I did an exceptional job of raising my daughter, but I would have to say it's because of who she is that made it so easy. She was a true privilege to raise, a joy, and she still inspires me every day. Yes, I had taken an old, broken-down sheep farm and transformed it into a beautiful retreat centre with hundreds of volunteers and a lot of money. But, somewhere inside, I knew there was more, so much more that I came here to experience and deliver.

Despite my determination not to get sucked in, this concept of highest and best and the calibre of people involved stirred something in me, and I felt drawn to listen to more of the audio clip. I heard the story of cutting-edge products and about the lives of these visionary leaders, which also tweaked my curiosity. The more I listened, the more I felt this sinking feeling in my gut. I suddenly knew I had to go to Portland. Chrystalle also encouraged me to go and check it out. She was particularly interested in the products.

At first, I felt mad . . . bloody hell . . . Renee Beth got me! Less than a week later, I found myself driving the seven hours down to Portland from Bowen Island.

She felt ecstatic that I would finally meet her team, and although I remained sceptical and wondered what I was getting myself into, I felt compelled to check it out.

Upon entering this large convention centre, which must have held thousands of people, I nearly turned and bolted. I decided to sit at the back of the room for a quick escape, when Renee Beth spotted me and came running over, thanked me for coming, and ushered me to my chair. I felt completely and utterly taken by judgment as I looked at the people there and thought them unhealthy, phoney, losers for attending. I can't believe I've admitted that, but that's what judgment looks like.

I solemnly vowed to myself I wouldn't get involved in any way other than as a customer. Talk about resistance. Little did I know I sat on the precipice of a brand-new life.

Within a short period, in fact, within forty-five minutes, I found myself moving out of my perched position and into a more relaxed, comfortable and especially open place. I started to feel pleasantly surprised with the vibe in the room and the phenomenal speakers . . . not the usual hype and rah-rah-rah.

During the break, I looked around and this time actually saw the people in the audience. They seemed professional-looking, conscious people, and cheery. Wow, they all appeared so healthy and happy. I did have a chuckle as to how my vision and perception of these people had changed in just one hour, or was it that the room had emptied out and a new group of people entered? Amazing how projection works.

At the end of the event, I agreed I would give it a go and see what happened.

I wanted to know once and for all if relationship marketing actually worked. I knew the products were effective because I'd had my amazing experience with them, but I wanted to know if the business was viable.

From that point on, I simply went to work. On the way home, I made phone calls and stopped at a friend's home to share with them this new endeavour.

I adapted this new venture into my amalgam to see what I could co-create with a team of like-minded entrepreneurs. My mentors taught me how to work with my strengths—strengths I didn't know I had.

In the first several months I absorbed as much as I could and showed up at everything.

As a team, we achieved success quickly and won bonuses for promotions we didn't even know about. By the end of the first month my business had moved through three ranks and not only recovered my initial investment but doubled it.

Soon a wonderful tribe gathered around this mission and the momentum of the business carried us along a fast river of success. On Nov 8, 2006, my first-year anniversary in the business, I felt surprised with what was achieved.

The first thing is I had actually stuck with it for one full year without once trying to pull away — a big accomplishment in itself. Not that I hadn't stuck with things I believed in, like my retreat centre. It was that I didn't believe in the industry at first and especially didn't think I would like it.

The second achievement was I was already earning over $5,000 per month (part-time), and that was just the beginning. I had asked for more consistent jackpots in my life, and when I was earning between $15,000 - $20,000 per month with this endeavour it was like a jackpot every month, lasting years.

The third thing was I found myself leaping out of bed early in the morning. Not just because of the awesome products; what rocked my world was I got to witness the beautiful transformations in people's lives, in their health, emotions, and their relationships. So, I made the wise decision to put my retreat centre on the back burner for the next three years and focus entirely on this business.

I want to acknowledge my sponsor, Renee Beth Poindexter, for her superhuman commitment in nurturing and supporting her fledging team into wholeness and leading the charge with this new paradigm of doing relationship marketing. She travelled from Portland to Vancouver on a monthly basis in the beginning until we were able to host our own programs and lead ourselves. Over the next decade I was blessed to have won just about every award the company offered. I was invited into the Field Advisory Counsel and have served on it ever since. I was inducted into the Millionaire Club, having personally earned over one million dollars in the first few years. I was honoured with the company's highest award for Leadership, Integrity, and Service, and continued to be the number-one associate in Canada for fourteen years. I never in my wildest dreams would have imagined such success with something I had been so adamantly opposed to.

The biggest surprise of all was finding the perfect partnership and parallel path with my work of transformation. It fulfils my desire to serve others to awaken their greatest gifts and talents.

Angelyn with her beloved horse Khodo

Chapter Sixteen

WAKE-UP CALL

The darkest moment
may be the point
of greatest illumination

As my relationship marketing business grew more and more successful, my attention on Xenia became less and less, and the place suffered greatly. My intention had always been to return fully to Xenia, but I got caught in earning more and more money and telling myself this was serving my retreat centre. And financially it did, for over a decade, but at quite a high price. Xenia got neglected, set on the back burner, and I had a variety of different people running the office and painting it with their particular flavour.

I had a stark wake-up call one day when some guests summoned me to a meeting with them in the Gathering Space. I felt so out of touch with Xenia and a little worried about what they had to say.

What I gleaned before attending the meeting was our office had mixed up the date of their arrival. In our books we thought they were coming on Friday, but they had in fact booked to come on Thursday. So basically, we were not prepared for them when they showed up.

The person doing the housekeeping had not even started making the beds or cleaning the cabins. She tended to leave it to the last moment. The facilitators of the program told me they arrived to a total mess and there was nobody around; not a soul at the centre. The person supposedly in charge had gone away for most of the day, thinking the guests would come the next day. To my absolute embarrassment, these facilitators took it upon themselves to clean and prepare the space for their group arriving in the afternoon.

My home is up on the hill, out of view from the main retreat area, which is partly why I had no idea what was happening. But the greater reason was I was out of touch with my staff, hoping everything would be okay. I learned the hard way, hoping and trusting are completely different.

As I made my way down the hill to our meeting place, I walked around and saw how bad things had become. There was an old shabby white sheet pinned to the inside of the glass office door. Opening the door, I could see why it had been placed there, the mess was piled high. It looked like a hoarder's space; you could barely see the desk under the piles of papers, books and bits and pieces. My heart sank and a slight panic arose. *How could I have gotten so out of touch?*

This was a low point for me as the owner of this business. I had wrapped myself up in the other business hoping for the best. But, one year led to another, and before I knew it, I had lost sight of my real dream.

The four facilitators were direct with me while at the same time compassionate, which was more than I deserved.

It became another major turning point in my business and the day I came home again. I put my retreat centre back on the front burner of my life and took back control of it.

From that point forth, I had my hand on the pulse of everything happening there. I found new people to manage the office and do the housekeeping. Pretty soon Xenia became more and more beautiful and presentable and, to this day, I feel in awe of what it has become. Instead of the rooms being cleaned and set for the next group just before they arrive, they are done promptly, the moment the groups leave. Even if we do not have a group for another week. I check them often and they are always impeccable.

It was a weird phenomenon; until I had earned my first million dollars with this RM Company, I couldn't truly own Xenia, my retreat centre. It felt like my poor husband had to die for my dream to be fulfilled, and there was a disconnect in embracing it fully.

I understand now why many people who win the lotto or receive large inheritances lose it *tout de suite.* I had proven I could earn my own money, and this changed my perspective and ability to receive. I started to learn even more deeply how important receiving is.

Xenia now offers a beautiful sanctuary in nature where people come from around the world to experience extraordinary silence and deep healing. Writers come to write, and couples come to get married in this pristine environment.

I have been able to build a barn that had sat incomplete for years. Our horses and guests love its gorgeous turquoise roof. We managed to fix the road, build new gates, repair some of the buildings, and give much-needed attention to this worthy place after years of neglect from my lack of loving attention and energy.

And joy of all joys, finally I gave myself time to write books. I am grateful for the time freedom and the ability to pay for a team to help me.

I cannot believe my life today—I wake up in gratitude and go to bed in gratitude—and what I love most of all is I have found the best mechanism for change and transformation I have ever seen, and you get paid to do it. My relationship marketing business now has a life of its own and doesn't require as much from me yet remains highly successful. I never would have imagined the fulfilment I would find.

My daughter had a sparkle in her eye when she said, "Mum, who would have ever thought you would find your dharma in relationship marketing?" We turned and looked at each other and burst into laughter. It just seemed so funny and unexpected.

In and of itself, it is not my Dharma, but it is part of my Dharmic Path to evolve. It is part of my overall vision. It has supported my retreat centre from going back to the bank, and it has helped so many people. For the record, the company that I have been committed to for all these years is called Univera, and if you would like to find out more, please visit my website and you will learn all about it.

I have realised that a jackpot isn't just about money; in fact, it is about a whole lot more. It is about the love and community in everyday living. I am grateful for this grace.

Have I achieved my highest and best yet? No way. Perhaps it's not a destination but a journey. But I do strive to live as my highest and best in all that I do.

Chapter Seventeen

FRIENDS FOREVER

Pure heart
your spirit speaks
so silently
thank you for
coming
in your wholeness

My friendship with Chrystalle unfolded like no other I had experienced. It grew into a mutual camaraderie imbued with reciprocity, rare and spiritually deep. I always thought I got the better end of the deal, and she always thought she did. We were total opposites in just about every way. When I first met Chrystalle in 1986, she rode a motorbike and slept on a bedroll. She dressed plainly but sure knew how to make beautiful cabinets. Woodworking was one of her passions. We always laughed when we said: the chances of us meeting and becoming close friends, was less than zero. Such opposites, she taught me how to use a hammer, and I taught her how to put on some makeup.

Together, we became a solid team in unfolding Xenia's mission along with Diane, Chrystalle's sister, other community members, and hundreds of volunteers. Chrystalle played a significant role in my daughter's life as her godmother. She taught her how to swim, ski, bake, bike, drive the tractor, and drive a car when she got older. Our friendship was unique, and we definitely connected at the soul level. If any such a thing as past lives exist, I feel sure we have lived many together. We finished each other's sentences, and whenever I thought, "Chrystalle, phone me," the phone would ring.

After twenty-five years of friendship, I lost my best friend. Sadly, Chrystalle left this world on October 1, 2010, at only sixty-one years of age. Way too soon for me, and for all of us. Along with Chrystalle's family, my daughter and I were with her for the last ten days and nights, holding vigil in palliative care. My daughter wouldn't leave her beloved godmother's side. It was difficult for her and very re-stimulating from the loss of her father. Chrystalle's death left quite a hole in our hearts, and we missed her terribly.

About a year after she died, I got to wondering how I could make contact with her. I thought if anyone could communicate from the other side of the veil, she could. I would go around my home and the land and say, "Chrystalle, where are you?"

One day, I came back from a trip and turned on my TV to watch a show I had recorded on my PVR. I noticed Rachael Ray had been recorded. That seemed odd because I hadn't programmed her show, but I thought maybe somebody staying at my house had, so I did some asking around. The reason it felt so significant was Chrystalle had loved Rachael Ray and bought nearly all her books. Turns out nobody had programmed Rachael Ray onto my PVR, but there it sat, as plain as day. I remember thinking, *Chrystalle, stop playing with my technology.*

Later the same night, while flicking through TV, I saw *Top Gun* was on and felt compelled to watch it again. I'm sure you will remember this movie with Tom Cruise as a fighter pilot. I sat watching the scene where Maverick (Tom Cruise) and Goose (Anthony Edwards) went on a drill mission when their plane got into trouble, and they had to get out of the cockpit in flight. As Goose ejected out of the plane, he banged his head on the way out, and they found him dead at the bottom.

Maverick was devastated because he had relied on his co-pilot for many years and many assignments. He had become deeply attached to his support and didn't think he could fly a mission without him. As you remember, in the movie, there came a time where he was asked to go out on a real live combat mission with another co-pilot. He said he couldn't go, and he was unable to do it without Goose.

As I watched this scene, I felt a resonance and knew I felt the same way about losing Chrystalle. I didn't know if I could go on with Xenia and our vision without her unconditional support. We were partners in crime and complimented each other's gifts and skills and personality. She was my Goose, my co-pilot.

The next morning, a person from my office came up to my house and gave me a photo she'd found as she cleared out some files. I was intrigued to see it. It was Chrystalle as a co-pilot when she flew with a pilot friend over Xenia taking pictures of our Labyrinth.
I got shivers all through my body when I saw the  image. Wow, coincidence or what?
In the afternoon, I was having a massage with Janie, our awesome, intuitive angel massage therapist. Out of the blue, she said, "Chrystalle is trying to get your attention."

I responded with, "You don't say! She's even tampered with my technology." And then I told her about *Top Gun* and Goose.

Janie said, "Let's tune in and see what message she has for us."

Shortly after relaxing and asking for the communication, I heard as clear as a bell, "I am still your Goose. I am just more effective from this place. Haven't you noticed?"

I got to thinking about the new people showing up at Xenia to help, the expansion of my relationship marketing business, the quickening of renovations and the clean-up, and I could feel Chrystalle working with them and encouraging them to get the job done. In fact, even years later, we continue to clean up and show up in ways so beautiful to behold, and Chrystalle remains, very much a part of it all. She always controlled and acted as the manager on the job site, and she wanted things to get cleaned up and all the tools put away afterward. There are many stories of people feeling literally managed by Chrystalle as she guides them from the other side.

In many ways, she became my courage and gave me the confidence to say, "Yes, let's do it." That's the kind of role she played in our friendship and in my work life. Her legacy lives on at Xenia, and I often think of her when we have completed another great task, knowing for sure she would have been thrilled.

I know Chrystalle was behind what happened next at Xenia. The community grew, and when I decided to put out a request for the person who was to manage Xenia and take care of our guests, Chrystalle, I'm sure, was involved with the hiring. That's when Saria showed up at Xenia.

Chrystalle and Saria definitely had the same quality of ethereal presence; they are other-worldly in a way. Both open minded to my seemingly crazy ideas, even when it didn't make sense on paper. When I reflect back, they should have said no to me so many times and put their foot down, but other than only a couple of incidences, it was always "Yes . . .okay, let's do it." I want to add neither one of them was a Pollyanna. It's just we had established a trust factor from our listening to guidance from the very beginning.

Saria has a fairy-like quality about her, and all our guests simply love interacting with her, either on the phone or in person at the retreat centre. I want to share about the radical trust she has endured over the past couple of years, which included her crusade with cancer (which she won).

Saria and I developed over time the same kind of serendipity that Chrystalle and I had. We also finished each other's sentences. Saria holds the hearth of Xenia strong in her management role as well as in her catering and healing sessions. I cannot say enough about how grateful I am to have her at my side on this mission of

Xenia. Saria also feels a connection with Chrystalle even though they never met in the physical. Sometimes she even feels managed by her.

Dale showed up at Xenia just before Chrystalle departed from this physical world, but he had a connection with her and also feels like he receives instructions from her at times. Dale has been a godsend to me and Xenia and is definitely an angel . . . a humble, very creative man who is always in service with all that he does.

Mike joined the team for four years, and he transformed so much of the infrastructure of Xenia and renovated the big yurt to include opening windows and a wooden exterior. He transformed an old wood-burning sauna into the magical Sanctuary we now call the Oracle, and although he wasn't exactly on the same page as many of us at the centre, he had an uncanny way of infusing beauty and pure energy into all that he created. He would not take credit for that very easily because it wasn't something he set about doing.

I know Chrystalle sent Mike to help us as well, and I will always feel blessed by the people that come and join our community and how Xenia always calls in what and who she needs and how sometimes she calls you by name.

And when precious friends leave their physical presence behind, it is concerning to the part of us believing in separation.

I have lost many precious friends, family and community members, and animals, and people wonder why I am not devastated by the loss. I do miss the physical presence, but I have radical trust in the continuum of all life.

Of course, it is always sad losing the physical presence of loved ones, and I was fortunate to be with many people and animals as they passed. I feel it is a real privilege to be part of this important passage.

Matthew, friend and wonderful builder of many of our creative gates at Xenia, had been sick for a couple of years and chosen every step of his dying experience, including what he wanted shared at his Celebration of Life event at Xenia after he passed. It was remarkable to be able to talk with him about dying so openly and consciously.

> *Until we can make peace with death, we can never live fully. This belief in separation we have been taught, is fraudulent.*

A week before Matthew passed, we had a beautiful conversation about his present perspective. I knew he was in a surrendered state, as he shared his experience through the eyes of an eagle he had meditated with. The eagle was on a tree outside his beloved cabin, overlooking the ocean. Matthew shared with me how he was starting to experience the non-separation state and how everything was simply particles and waves of energy. During his meditation with the eagle, he asked if he could see through its eyes. Instantly, Matthew was able to see through the waves and deep into the ocean, as an eagle would. It was profoundly spectacular how he was given this sight. It made clear how an eagle could swoop down from a tree and clutch a salmon into its talons with upmost precision. I loved hearing this story and feeling the love and acceptance resonating through Matthew.

Five days later I was summoned to his house to receive a book he wanted me to read. His body frail but his spirit still very present, he gave me instructions and the book. We shared a few gentle words before he closed his eyes again.

The next day, I was called by Deb, Matthew's wife, along with our dear sister Ellen, to come for an hour or so to meditate and pray with her. I'm not surprised Ellen and I were called in together because we are often called in for important soul assignments.

Arriving at their home, I realized this wasn't for a meditation but to help usher dear Matthew home. He lay on his bed, still, labouring with the dying breath. The angelic music playing in the room captivated my soul. It was a beautiful recording Matthew and Deb produced a few years earlier. The chants were making my body quiver with joy.

Chris, Matthew's best friend of over thirty-seven years, was pleased to have us arrive. Ellen and I settled on Matthew's bed beside Deb. After a few gentle words were spoken, we moved into a meditation and absorbed the songs and love in the space. Chris stepped back to the door so he could observe us women doing our end-of-life doula work with Matthew.

I have to say, it was powerful and perfect as the sun was setting on the ocean right behind us. We sang and prayed and shared thoughts with Matthew as he had already slipped into a deep state. There was a lightness and joy present and an intense feeling of love. A few times we thought Matthew had gone but another breath transpired and we continued to meditate together. All of a sudden, I had the thought that perhaps he would want to take his last breath alone, as I have heard many souls do.

I shared how Matthew may want some space and for us to leave the room, being a fearlessly independent person. Chris, Ellen and I left the room to make tea and shortly afterwards Deb joined us saying she wanted to give him the opportunity to be alone as well.

Grabbing two long, red candles from a bookshelf, Deb put them on the fireplace to light them. It took her half a dozen matches for them to actually light, but when they did, she looked behind into the bedroom where Matthew lay and she said, "I think he is gone." We all rushed in and surrounded him as he shuddered slightly. and then released one last breath.

A dear friend, husband, brother, uncle, creative spirit and infinite being was gone from this reality and popped into another. Matthew, being the prolific creator of many songs, paintings and words, leaves a huge legacy of his expression behind. He had impacted many people's lives with his spirit and friendship.

Since Matthew and I had a common interest in listening to guidance, as shared in his book, *The Soul Knows, A Path of Listening,* we had previously arranged ways to communicate after he passes. We didn't know exactly what form this would take but we mused with a few ideas. The next day Matthew's body was taken from the tiny cabin, and Ellen and I returned to assist Deb in the whole process of clearing any discordant energy from the illness lingering in the cabin and bringing forth gratitude and love. We helped her remake her bed with fresh linen and smudged and sang into her room.

I noticed that morning since awaking I had a strong ringing in my right ear. It was loud and consistent. At first, I thought maybe I had hurt my ear or something, but soon I realised Matthew was trying to get my attention. Back home in the afternoon, I was sitting at my dining room table looking at the eternal candle from the Sanctuary when I focussed in on the ringing sound in my ear.

I tuned in to see if I could connect with Matthew's message. Right away it came as clear as a bell. *Open the Sanctuary!* the message insisted.

I had literally closed the Sanctuary for repairs the day before, which is why the eternal candle was at my house and not the Sanctuary.

Tossing out an old bedraggled rug we placed a new one in there but kept it rolled up until the leak on the roof was fixed. I estimated the Sanctuary would be closed for about a month. Well, here's what happened:

A friend of mine came over just as I was putting up the closed sign on the Sanctuary door. He volunteered to come back the next day to fix the leaks in there. Since Matthew had a very close connection to the Sanctuary, he wanted it to be a place available for people to come and offer blessings and feel a sense of connection to him during this grieving time.

So off I went with Elinor and opened the Sanctuary, cleaning it up and rolling down the new beautiful carpet. I brought the eternal candle back and lit it, with gratitude for Matthew's clear messages. Later I added a photo of Matthew and kept it there until his Celebration of Life ceremony.

Reporting this message about the Sanctuary to Deb and Ellen in their kitchen that evening, Deb said, "Listen," and motioned for me to pay attention to the music playing in the background. It was Matthew singing his song "Sanctuary".

Over the following days and weeks there was a spectacular show of humpback whales and hummingbirds outside the window of Matthew's cherished cabin. Deb shared the delight she felt and the recognition of her husband's spirit rejoicing and sending back acknowledgements of freedom and joy.

The understanding that we are not separate, and nothing is separate was deepening with every experience and lesson unfolding upon the path.

Aerial shot of Xenia's Labyrinth taken by co-pilot, Chrystalle.

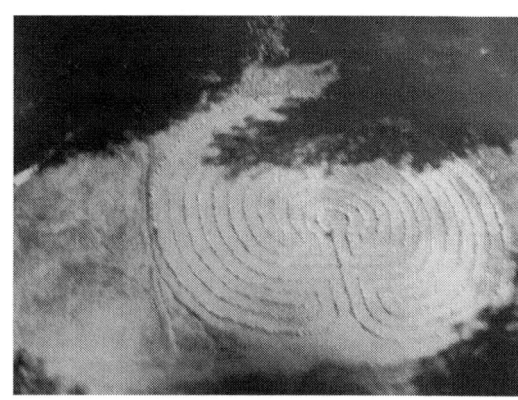

*Money is for creating
environments
within which
the experience of
money cannot buy.*[9]

---

[9] This statement came from a Vancity document

Chapter Eighteen

SERVING A VISION

*Being of Service
is giving and receiving
simultaneously*

From the very beginning, Xenia has had a magical energy, and even the most sceptical feel it right away. In the twenty-five years I have owned this land, I have watched it transform from an old dilapidated sheep farm into a glorious thirty-eight-acre sanctuary where thousands of people from around the world have had this exact experience that money cannot buy. Our guest books continue to be filled with people's gratitude and experiences of feeling deeply at home.

Until now, our guests have varied from corporate executives to street kids recovering from drugs to, actors, singers, authors, counsellors, spiritual seekers and other individuals from all walks of life. They report having had profound, life-changing results and experiences while staying at Xenia. Not only does Xenia offer her magic through nature, including OPA, the meadows, and forested valley, but also our beloved horses, Khodo and Major, Tofino the donkey, and Mars the miniature horse, who intermingles with and delights our guests. And of course, Gracie, my loving and intelligent labradoodle, who simply loves on the people at the retreat. Many of our animals live long and healthy lives at Xenia. Sanderman, one of our horses, lived to be thirty-four years old. Billy, our adorable Lab, lived to sixteen and Charlie, our beloved piggy, lived nearly sixteen years with us and passed away in 2019. He left us and his major fan club of guests behind. His presence will be greatly missed.

The reason Xenia holds such presence is it has been loved and cared into existence by hundreds of people's efforts over the decades.

What a true labour of love this project Xenia has proven to be. Thousands of people have graced our land by their presence, and you can feel the love when you enter. As I define our brand, I come up with the word *Nothing*. Yes, that's right, nothing more than is needed for a safe, creative, and wonderful experience. Most people who visit report a feeling of home and tranquillity as they leave the residue of city life behind for a short while.

I have protected Xenia from becoming cluttered with dogma or themes and cherish the nothingness we have. It lends itself to fill in with potentiality from guests upon their unique journey. I understand, from a marketing point of view, offering *Nothing* may not attract crowds, but somehow, I know the soul that seeks this space for rest and play will understand right away of what I speak.

The glue that holds our community together is the deep sense of purpose and love felt with every group and person who comes. Though we each have different roles to play, we know our presence is significant.

WORKING WITH TEENAGERS AND YOUNG ADULTS

I cherished the programs we did with young adults, and boy, did they teach us so much. We did magical programs combining youth living on the street and youth who came from wealthy homes. Some kids arrived in their own Jeeps with cell phones and all the props money could provide, and others arrived from organizations like Covenant House, a place that supports street kids. They had one thing in common, and that was their recovery from drug abuse. Our programs focussed particularly on creativity and communications.

I always marvelled at how separate and judgemental the kids started out and by the end there was no separation about who had what or came from where. They bonded at such a heart level as they witnessed each other's journeys.

Opening Pathways of Awareness is what this work with teenagers is all about, and I love it as much as I loved working with spirited horses in my early years.

Transformation happened to them around their ability to be in nature without all the usual props and typical technological entertainment. Instead, we developed the art of connection and savoured the creativity arising out of the space of safety.

I noticed in my work with teenagers that when I applied the same principles I had learned from horses and natural horsemanship, a beautiful trust and openness occurred. The relationship with teenagers demanded gentleness, honesty and spaciousness to develop any kind of trust and safety.

We have learned you don't break a horse's spirit, as in the old paradigm of getting control over a horse, but instead you join up with them. This means with respect and grace, not control and power. You command respect, not demand it, which has a very different quality.

You don't go out and catch the horse who wants to be free and wild; instead you let it catch you. And most importantly, you leave your ego at the gate before entering their domain.

The same is true with teenagers. You cannot control them, and the more you try, the more you alienate them and send them away. There was only one irrefutable rule in my household, and that was respect. Respect was the pinnacle upon which everything else was built. After that I was able to say "yes" most of the time.

Teenagers have less if any desire to please adults, unlike the younger age group. They are sorting out who they are apart from the indoctrination they have received. Their programming and conditioning have racked havoc with their spirits, and we wonder why they are known as rebellious. The last thing they want is for some well-meaning adult to inflict their pearls of wisdom upon them. Who said it is wrong to make mistakes anyway, to fall down the hole in the road as many times as is needed to become aware? Who said pain was bad?

We all have our own destiny, and teenagers are no exception. Our only job is to hold out a safe container to be available whenever they need us so they can catch us. Don't give too much eye contact or too much attention – let them have their space but be there when they need us even if we cannot see it openly. Look for the subtle clues that say, "It's okay to say something kind to me . . .it's okay to love and hug me, but not too much and not in front of my friends and please back off when I have had enough."

On one retreat, we had some of the roughest street kids. Some were coming off drugs, and one young man was on his way to a detention facility. As they arrived, I made a point of being around but not overly attentive or welcoming. One girl in particular had an attitude and clearly was incredibly angry at being sent to the retreat. I understand her mother bribed her with money and cigarettes if she would attend. She was there to kill time but not to participate, and she made that painfully clear. I watched her for the first couple of days but at the corner of my eye, so as not to intrude.

On the third day I could see she was curious, wondering *who is this woman who owns this place? She's not saying very much.* I could tell she wanted to connect with me, but I didn't approach her. Then one evening at the fire pit, I sat down beside her on a log, still not engaging with her directly but simply sitting and looking out at the fire. Soon she started talking with me, and that was it. The join-up had happened. From then on, she trusted me, and we created a strong bond and platform upon which she could trust. It took a while; in fact, three out of the ten days we were together, but that was how long it took. During those three days she had created a lot of stress in the group, but I knew if I took my time, I could really connect with her.

THE MAGIC OF THE HORSE

For many years our horses roamed freely at Xenia and when I think of it now, it was both magical and downright imprudent (from a liability point of view).

I would get phone calls from neighbours saying the horses were on their lawn or they were down by the houses overlooking a high cliff to the ocean. Sometimes it was dark when we went out looking for them.

There are two reasons I let this happen. One was because of the miraculous experiences that happened spontaneously with our guests and the horses. Also, I mentioned Instinx in earlier chapters, and well, I was instinctively in a place the Tarot Card would address as The Fool . . . and what a blessing it was that we never had a bad incident. There were times when Tango, my daughter's beautiful black, rather large thoroughbred went charging through a group of unsuspecting guests at a flat-out gallop.

On the positive side, there were so many inspiring stories of healings and magic happening with our guests. One lady was a burned-out CEO from Alberta who came to rest, having suffered from depression from years of stress. One day she was sitting on the bench outside, Maple Cottage in her summer sandals when Beau, my daughters Percheron horse with massive hooves, approached her. She said he pulled her forward with his head and kept it there on her back for a few moments before he bowed his head to her chest, eventually walking off. Then the two other horses greeted her as if to check on his work and off they all went down the trail. She said she was blown away but not afraid. From that day forth her energy brightened up and before she left, she was happy.

Another time we had a guest walking towards the Labyrinth and she was afraid of the horses, hoping she would not see them on her travels. Sure enough, there they were, head to butt, sleeping on the side of the road. At first she panicked and wanted to turn back but gradually as she stood there, she felt the urge to take the opportunity to grow. She plucked up the courage to take a wide birth and go around them. Of course, Tango woke up and followed her down the dirt pathway. She thought surely, he wouldn't come into the Labyrinth, and she scurried into the centre of it. When she turned around, there he was right behind her. This beautiful black creature stood there offering his love and presence.

Telling us the story later, she said she couldn't believe how her fear dissolved and she was able to stay present with him for a while. Afterwards, she ran back down the hill and asked me if she could groom him. There was a transformation for her that day, and her fear of horses fell away. And I am sure it released other fears she may have had as well.

I could go on and on with examples of how the horses interacted with our guests, including trying to get into the lodge. Can you imagine arriving and having to move a horse out of the way before you can enter? *I know, it's not for everyone.* I loved the freedom we could give the horses and how they were able to take  part in the events happening at Xenia, but there came a time when it became clear we needed to build fenced paddocks for them to keep  everyone safe. The guests could still visit them in their barn or the meadows. I did feel sad at first but knew it was the right thing to do.

Side bar: I'm presently in India where cows, horses, mules and dogs run freely and safely between the bustling cars, Tuk Tuks, motor bikes and buses. They all seem to have an understanding and an extraordinary prowess within this bedlam of activity.

I did not give up on having the horses do their healing work with our guests. This year we started working with the horses and our groups in communication programs.  Evelyn McKelvie, author of *The Professional Horse*,[10] led the first program and the energy was outstanding. Check out our website for photos. In 2020 I will be joining her in co-facilitating another program involving our herd.

I giggle when I think, *what were the chances of my daughter becoming an equine veterinarian*? HIGH. I loved how she was hooked on horses at a very young age the way I was, and we had many bonding times as we rode together through the trails. It was always an uplifting experience. And soon I will be holding her baby while she competes in reining shows next year or does her veterinary work with these magnificent creatures.

AH HA MOMENT:

One day I realised being had by a vision went back even further than I first realized. I discovered this connection in a guided meditation I was doing. After a

---

[10] Evelyn McKelvie https://equinecoach.ca/

wonderful surrender into the body and beyond, we were directed to visualize a beautiful meadow. Our guide prompted us: *Remember it is possible to create anything with your imagination. You can fly, swim or do anything you want. Now take some time to play and have fun in the meadow.*

Suddenly, I was standing atop one of our fields, looking at a beautiful sunny scene below. I noticed the barn reflecting light from its gorgeous teal metal roof. The donkey and miniature horse were happily grazing, and the two horses were in the fields beyond the barn. I swooped down (with my imaginary wings ☺) and picked up the donkey and carried him in my arms like a baby. Next I placed him outside his pen in a lovely grassy area. I played for a while, rearranging pens and fences, and my heart burst open with joy. It was a beautiful meditation, and I was inspired for the rest of the day.

In the afternoon I reflected on my childhood where I would spend hours in the toy shop with my pocket money, painstakingly choosing which tiny winy farm animal I was going to buy that week. For years I had collected a farm with horses, sheep, haystacks, barns, fences, goats, pigs and even a little dog. I would play for hours, moving the animals around, acting out various scenarios. It was my pride and joy and a precious gift I passed on to my daughter when she was old enough.

Next, I thought about my beautiful thirty-eight-acre retreat centre, Xenia, also a hobby farm. We have ponies, a donkey, a pig, horses, barns, fences, trees, rivers and many of the things I imagined as a child. (see image on back cover).

WOW....I am living this childhood dream. My farm had manifested from this hobby and dream as a child, and I hadn't quite seen the impact of this and the manifestation until now, in this beautiful meditation. I didn't deliberately or consciously set about creating a farm. In fact, growing up in England as a working-class member, the idea of actually owning anything would not have entered my head. Just like going to university wasn't in my vocabulary, but somehow a roadmap was set in place and my soul was following it.

I love how my work with manifestation was seeded a long time ago, and every day another piece of understanding sinks in. When a vision has you, it may have had you for a very long time.

VOLUNTEERS

Xenia has always drawn people who want to contribute to her mission one way or another. Some have volunteered for years, and I still marvel at their generosity. I have so much gratitude for the hundreds of volunteers who have graced this land and mission by their volunteering.

We have always said Xenia calls you, and sometimes calls you by name. Literally every time we need help and we put it out there, within hours we receive an email or phone call magically from a person looking to volunteer their time, and they usually have the skill base we are needing right at that particular moment.

Another example, and believe me, there are hundreds like this: I was moving heavy bales of hay at the barn with another lady but before we were finished, she had to leave in order to get her daughter to work on time.

I said, "No worries, you go, and I will find help later to complete the task." She reluctantly left, and as she was pulling out of the driveway, a man on a motorbike appeared at the barn.

"Hi," he said and took off his helmet. "Do you need a hand?" Before I could barely answer, he was off his bike and started lifting the very heavy bales all by himself. He was strong, willing and happy. It was cosmic how he showed up in that very second. It turned out he was staying on Bowen Island for the weekend and knew about Xenia so had decided to come over for a visit. I then realized he looked familiar and it turned out he was a new member of my Univera team. I gave him a tour of Xenia and had a wonderful interaction with him.

Oh, who is in charge of all this, anyway? *It is truly all handled.*

My niece was visiting from England one year and she said that I scared her and I was a witch because early one morning in the spring, I said to her, "Boy, do we need help here in the garden." Everything was totally overgrown because it hadn't been put to bed properly the previous year. It was full of weeds and long grass and dead vines.

Within two hours of my requesting help out loud, twelve men walked down the road and came over, thanking us for letting them walk the Labyrinth that day. They said they would like to give back and spend a couple of hours helping. What could they do?

Without any further ado we had all the rakes and forks and wheelbarrows ready to go. The next two hours were wonderful to behold as twelve strong, capable men turned over all the beds, added manure, cleared the whole thing and literally transformed the garden. That is when my niece thought I was some kind of witch. By the way, miracles happen all the time to all of us, if we pay attention.

Having a retreat centre is a labour of love and not usually a profitable endeavour. Just before buying Xenia, I remember going to Gabriola Island to a well-known

217

retreat centre to do my due diligence and establish the validity of such an enterprise. I wanted advice and opinions and made an appointment with the manager there.

It wasn't the response I expected. She literally tried every tactic to dissuade me from doing it. She said, "It is a lot of work, and you will never make any money."

Either she was having an off day, or she was down on the idea. I'm sure she wasn't worried about the competition I may have created. I think it was more that she was worn down.

It did put a damper on my spirit for a while, and I had to consider what she was saying, but I knew it wasn't about a business proposition in the usual terms. I knew from the very beginning it would be labour of love.

Many years later, having bought the land and well into the project, I was in a circle at the Gathering Yurt at Xenia and across the room I noticed a lady who felt familiar, yet I couldn't quite put my finger on where I had met her before. During the break she came over to me and introduced herself, saying, "Well, I am so glad you didn't take my advice; this place is truly magical." It was her.

Why has Xenia attracted so many volunteers? I myself am a volunteer, not that I set it up that way, but to this day, up until this year (2019) I have never received a paycheck from Xenia. Instead, I have always had to supplement the monthly expenses from my other businesses to Xenia. Over the years I have attempted to make it at the very least sustainable, and we are getting there. In fact, the past two years have been non-stop, one group in, one group out, so it is not that we are not earning the money, it's just a costly endeavour with staff and thirty-eight acres of land to maintain. I often wondered why I didn't take on partners who could inject more money into the project, but all along it seemed important to keep the reins in my own hands in order to honour the spirit of the land.

Even the people who work at Xenia for a minimum stipend and accommodation give way more than they financially earn.

I have noticed people love to volunteer, and they get so much out of it. It did cause me to ponder why people come and so willingly and generously give of their time and sometimes even their money. This is what I think happens:

- It is for a higher purpose
- It is a way to be in service as a spiritual quest
- It is fun and inspiring
- They became part of a co-creative community
- They can express themselves creatively
- They love being in nature

- They resonate with the brand of service offered
- They love the fellowship of working together
- They enjoy the physical activity and meals
- They are making an impact
- They leave a legacy for future generations

One time, one of our major helpers, Dale, said in regard to the volunteers, "You are very good at receiving, and I think this is why people want to help."

Yes, that is very true. I am good at receiving, especially for Xenia. Sometimes I think I am a receiving tower to help fund things like this project.

It is rewarding to work for something you consider significant and be of service and offer your heart and your hard work without motive or getting paid. I do believe in reciprocity, and it is very important to me. I make sure people are acknowledged and witnessed for their contribution as well as making sure they are fed and have a warm bed if they are staying over.

One day a friend said she wished she could get this kind of volunteer help at her place and she couldn't understand why I could and she couldn't. I said it wasn't about me, and that was why. In other words, it wasn't to me they were volunteering but to Xenia. Why would they volunteer and give so generously? Because they bought into the bigger vision and were allowed to enjoy the benefits of their labour.

From the very beginning I have made the Sanctuary, OPA and the Labyrinth available to the public as a giveback, but more importantly because in the early days of Xenia, an elderly couple were walking down the road. They spotted me leaving OPA, and knowing I was the new owner of the land, they asked if they could have permission to visit the tree they had been visiting for fifty years and grown fond of. It was in that moment I knew I had no right to keep people away from this sentient being, and I chose to open the specified areas up to the public.

Chapter Nineteen

ANGELS WANT TO HELP US

How can one person
be given so much
The gratitude is enormous
That's how come

I started to work more consciously with the Angels and Arch Angels, calling them in to help. And I became increasingly aware of Earth Angels, meaning people who are Angels in the physical form, here to help us. I noticed the flow and empowerment when I trusted this and remembered to ask not just once but continuously and asking on behalf of other people and situations. Asking and receiving are very important. Angels do not want to impose anything on us, so it is incumbent upon us to ask for help.

Whenever I have to speak on stage, I take a few moments ahead of time to quietly invite the Angels to assist me with the best message the audience needs to hear. The trick, of course, is to listen and then execute their message. I'm not talking about handing the whole thing over, but why not?

At one retreat I was facilitating for a young millionaire corporate team, I was preparing for their program and got really clear instructions to **not prepare**. At least, not in the usual way of painstakingly planning for weeks ahead. Instead I was to prepare by being present, open and available so I could be there for them and unfold the program as was called for in each moment. It's not that I don't know my stuff; it's about not over preparing and trusting I will know what to do at any given moment. This is the art of trusting in the highest order. I honoured this and simply sat with OPA, walked the Labyrinth, groomed the horses and walked my dog. Of course, the ego was screaming, *what are you doing, you had better prepare, you need a program, you are going to screw up. OMG, you will be in trouble.*

It wasn't easy, but I simply showed up at the retreat at a high level of presence, and it was wonderful. It was the best retreat ever, and I learned so much about trusting myself and calling upon the Angels.

Eckhart Tolle, teacher and author of *The Power of Now* and *A New Earth*, has a message that says, "To offer no resistance to life is to be in a state of grace, ease, and lightness." It's not about fixing anything or anyone but, instead, being present now.

After reading Eckhart's book *The Power of Now* for the fourth time and still not being able to explain its real meaning, I realised I comprehended it on a level beyond mind. In fact, it is the first book I have ever read defying logical meaning yet offering deep connection. It stirred something so deep inside me, I felt compelled to meet this teacher.

A friend in the States knew him personally, so I asked if he would introduce us. Within three days, I sat across from Eckhart in a restaurant, having brunch.

It felt a great blessing to meet with him. He was sweet, and I loved his simple, humble manner and genuine interest. After brunch, I gave him the photo album of Xenia and the work we did. Graciously, he looked through it with such attention and presence. He must have read every word on every page, though I meant only for him to flick through the pictures. I recognized the power of giving someone your full attention, even for just a moment—it gave a teaching in itself. While hugging him to take my leave, a powerful energy current passed through my entire body. Full of love, it didn't feel personal but universal.

I invited Eckhart to visit Xenia and he accepted, saying it would happen within a couple of months. After three months had passed, I called him to see if he still planned to visit, but I always got an answering machine. Perhaps he was on tour, as he had become so well-known and in high demand. One early morning, while sipping on my tea, I received a message to phone Eckhart. At first, I resisted, thinking I didn't want to leave yet another message and be a nuisance. Sipping on my second cup of tea, I heard it again: *Phone Eckhart now.*

Without further ado, I dialled his number, and, to my surprise, Eckhart picked up the phone. He sounded delighted to hear from me and we arranged for him to come over to Xenia.

I must say I felt nervous picking him up at the ferry, this famous man whose influence had transformed the consciousness of the planet. His books were unable to stay on bookshelves due to the high demand (every author's dream).

Before lunch, I gave Eckhart a tour of Xenia. We wove through the Labyrinth, visited the Sanctuary, continued along the forest paths and sat quietly in my home. We naturally fell into spontaneous periods of silence. At one point, as we were meditating across from each other in my living room, I watched Eckhart disappear, and the house around us disappear, and all I could see were waves of energy. Everything seemed to merge into one. We were no longer separate forms.

I got to see how we are not just our body, and later, I asked him about this transmission of energy. Eckhart said he had not transmitted the energy but, as we sat together,

225

the transmission happened because of the two of us, like when two or more are gathered.

Simple things seemed to bring great joy to Eckhart. For instance, my cat Magic, who purred in bliss as Eckhart stroked him. He said Magic was the real teacher here. I loved spending this day with Eckhart; he is a true and authentic teacher who lives in the Now. As I drove back from the ferry later that afternoon, I knew I had been touched deeply, and I knew the importance of our work of stillness.

Another very important teacher who visited Xenia was Dorothy Maclean, co-founder of Findhorn in Scotland who worked with the Angels and Elemental Kingdom. Dorothy came to do a workshop with us and connected with the elemental kingdom at Xenia, saying this place was chosen a long time ago and has an ordained role. She particularly loved OPA and shared how important and misunderstood the role of the ancient trees are in our lives, how they carry the wisdom and messages from the Universe. As well, the energy and work they are doing is invisible to us but

profound in its effect. She also loved Charlie, our potbelly pig. He was only a little guy at that time.

I don't know if angels really exist, but it is a wonderful idea and powerful morphic field. I know there is a huge angel overseeing Xenia, and I have directly experienced it. It is my belief and it works for me. I invite you welcome them into your life and see what happens. I'd love to hear your stories.

READING THE MESSAGES AND SIGNS

Observing people has interested me since I was a small child. I would always people watch and listen to what they said, and more particularly to what they did. This fascination followed me through my whole life, into my teams and communities I lived and worked with. My enquiry was: *why do some people succeed and some do not – even with similar circumstances?* This definitely was why Instinx attracted me and why after a decade into my relationship marketing business I noticed patterns and beliefs with people's behaviours in my team, which informed my creation of *From Squeak to Roar—Unleashing the Potential in your Relationship Marketing Tribe.*[11] This book looks at how people do relationship marketing,

---

[11] From Squeak to Roar – Unleashing the potential in your Relationship Marketing Tribe - angelyntoth.com or amazon.ca

identified through seventeen different animals and their characteristics.

As I finished up writing *From Squeak to Roar*, one thing felt incomplete and was nagging at me. I kept receiving whispers that I had to add lynx to the collection of animals, but I refused, not seeing how it related. How do people do RM as the Lynx? One day, I received a phone call at my office declaring a huge dead wild cat lay at OPA. Saria and one of our volunteers and I ran up to see. I was praying it wasn't my cat Raj. To our total amazement it was a dead lynx sitting there on the knee of

OPA. Clearly someone must have dropped off this magnificent lynx, as they are not found on Bowen or within hundreds of miles of there. It had been placed on the knee of OPA with  a little smudge pot beside it. I don't think it had been dead too long, and it looked as if it had gotten trapped or injured. We called the police in to investigate whether it came down to some weird prank or "offering," and both the police who attended, along with the three of us, felt it harmless and had simply been placed in our Sanctuary as a place where it would be honoured and buried. Perhaps someone found it off-island and thought it should come to Xenia. I guess we'll never know the truth, but one thing for sure, it provided me with full awareness of this message of the lynx.

Regardless, I still refused to add lynx to the mix, brushing it off as a coincidence. However, I did become a little intrigued and researched more about them. To my utter amazement, I found I related to its characteristics way more than I ever would have imagined. In fact, it echoed how I did my business so successfully. These resplendent and lucid creatures serve the invisible rules of the game. They understand the act of doing less and achieving more by purposeful actions. Still, no way would I make myself that vulnerable and add it to the book. Even more so, now I had identified myself as "the Lynx."

Three nights later, I got woken in the middle of the night with a message and clear instruction: *Go to your office and write out your Skype name.*

What? ... No way.

I tried to go back to sleep.

Yes, get up and write out your Skype name, came the instructions from my higher Self.

I dragged myself out of bed and wrote out the Skype name I had for over five years on a piece of paper—it was a combination of my name and Xenia's name. Promptly, I went back to bed and slept.

In the morning, I was curious about it and went back to my office and looked at the piece of paper and there, as plain as day, I saw it in my skype name: ange**lynx**enia. Lynx got added to my book immediately.

Life speaks to all of us every day and all-day long, sometimes in metaphor, sometimes in messages. We can safely know a higher power guides us if we can simply tune in and act upon the messages. It takes courage to begin, and radical trust to continue.

PART THREE – THE POWER OF SILENCE

Chapter Twenty

AMBASSADOR OF THE SOUL

The soul loves sun naps
The ego says: It is such a waste of time
But since time does not exist
go ahead

It would take many, many years before I stood fully in my purpose of being the Ambassador of the Soul. There, I said it before I closed this book. That is my passion, and that is what I am interested in. I no longer care about feeding the ego personality and helping people find monetary or material success. Not that there is anything wrong with it; there are so many teachers taking care of the "manifesting abundance" department.

Why the soul and what is the soul? What are soulful things to do and achieve? In the simplest sense, it is that which brings you joy. By honouring your Calling, you are honouring your soul. By living my art, I am living as the soul. By riding my horse and walking my dog, I am being my soul. By falling into the silence, I AM the soul. Writing my books to you, I am honouring my soul. The soul doesn't care about going to the gym, frantic diets or making money for the sake of it. The soul feels it all and relishes the depth of emotion and expression.

SERVING THE SOUL THROUGH THIS VISION OF XENIA HAS BECOME MY GREATEST HONOUR.

I can feel how much it was meant to be and how guided the process has been and continues to be. All the insecurity about who I thought I was to do this has long gone. The doubt that perhaps I had just made up the Vision and I didn't really receive guidance has settled into a gentle and calm peace.

The silent retreats have formed into a unique and powerful process we call The Vigil. It involves courage and willingness to turn within and listen to the inner guidance. I will not give the process away of how it works because it is better to experience it, but we are getting rave reviews from people, and here are just a couple of the many testimonials:

1 / In Silence, I found My Voice.

When the noise of my life threatened to drown me out, I found myself at a crossroads — sad and feeling trapped and helpless. I knew I needed solace and space to reflect, to find my way forward. Xenia Silent Retreat provided that place for me and came at the exact right time in my life. That first night during our opening circle, I set the intention for peace. I came away from the silent retreat with much more than peace. I came away with a voice connected to my deepest and highest good and a clarity for how to make that happen now, and in the future. A transformation that my husband and my daughter see . . . but most importantly, that I feel down to my bones.

The person who arrived at Xenia Friday night was not the person who left on Sunday. Fear, doubt, sadness, helplessness dropped away, and in its place is a sense of deep compassion for myself with a commitment and understanding of how important and necessary taking care of self is.

Diane

2/ I was able to truly be present to myself and connect to the beauty of Xenia in ways that truly took me on an evolutionary shift in my awareness-I felt more connected to Nature, and through my time walking the Labyrinth and to Angel's Landing as well as Honeymoon Lake I could feel I was deepening my trust in myself and my connection to a higher counsel. As I let go of my mental focus and free fell into the spiritual realm through trusting Nature in a way that I didn't even know was possible, it has catapulted me into a new place. So thank you for being the catalyst! You have created an amazing experience for people to come home to themselves, and what a ripple effect that can generate... Renee Beth

Xenia attracts people from all over the world. Considering we have not advertised or marketed in any significant way, we always feel surprised at how people find their way to this little ten-kilometre Island in the Pacific at the far reaches of Western Canada. People come from Australia, Japan, China, Germany, Hawaii, and of course, the US, England, and many other places. This one group flew in from Asia for a one-week program. They were, apparently, business owners with busy lives, and the work was to help them find silence and nature again. I was invited into their finishing circle followed by a full-moon candlelit Labyrinth walk. Although I had observed them throughout the week coming and going, I didn't know much about their culture and protocols. So, I felt a little nervous to enter their final circle. The organizers invited me as a surprise to their group.

I arrived in the Gathering Space at 8:30 p.m., as instructed. Twenty people sat in a circle in a beautifully lit space. Flowers and soft lights and candles created warmth and safety. They asked me to share my story of establishing Xenia, and through a translator, I spoke the stories contained in this book.

Tears and gratitude flowed like nothing I had ever seen before in a group. My story touched and inspired them to live their dreams at a higher level. Next, the eagle feather got passed around as each person shared their experience of staying at Xenia. I heard from a man who had stood at OPA and after holding a secret for thirty-five years, shared it with the tree and then sobbed and literally wailed so loud he released all his pain. There was such a bright light in his eyes as he shared how renewed and hopeful he felt. Each participant had connected profoundly to the land and spirit of Xenia, and as a result, connected more deeply to themselves and their true nature.

As I listened to the stories through their tears of joy and gratitude, I could not stop appreciating how important this whole project of building Xenia and going the distance was, even if only for what had happened with this group and these gentle folk who are the same as me, yet sit on top of an ancient culture. We may have different ethos, but it became evident to me that night that *we are one*. We have the same insecurities and dreams, and we all deserve love and respect. The love in the Gathering Space grew palpable, and before we left to go to the Labyrinth, they sang me a song in their native tongue. It was precious, and I will always remember how honoured I felt by these people.

We travelled together in silence, and it brought a breath-taking moment when we came upon the Labyrinth, lit up for us ahead of time with candles. Right overhead hung the full moon, peering into this otherwise dark field, surrounded by a circle of large trees holding the space. While we stood at the gateway, ready to go in, a beautiful big deer walked by, glowing from the light of the moon. I could see and feel the awe of this moment in their faces as the group entered the Labyrinth one by one. The light and sound of the night with the crickets, frogs, and even the owl calling, filled the senses to perfection. My heart burst with love and gratitude while I witnessed the presence of this group walking the pathways of the Labyrinth, gently singing on the way out, and peace filled my heart and the entire space.

It touched me more than any other time because I understood in the experience just how similar we all are at the core of our hearts and souls. I realised that night I will always be guided to do whatever it takes to maintain this creation of Xenia and why its legacy must live on. This group came back often after

> "Your Vigil Silent Retreat is your *sine qua non*, and perhaps the signature event that highlights the gifts of Xenia so well."
> Matthew Smith

that, and they have asked to translate my book into their language.

After twenty-four years of leading the silent retreats, I started to understand at a far deeper level the impact of this program. People feel the silence enter the space and it became my study.

Finding Silence, Finding Self
Out of the silence I AM and from this knowing life continues
on through me in ways that flow forward and release me from
the burden of having to choose and effort this life. I can sit back
down as the silence, since this is who I really am. The silence.

In the original vision I was asked to introduce the work of silence in every program and all that we do. As a result, I made sure other facilitators understood the vast gift Xenia was offering their group, if they would remember to use the silence and nature as part of their program. I certainly added plenty of silence into my writing retreats and other programs and found out the importance of setting up the program with soul writing.

When a new group arrives, the participants usually want to get to know each other with all the usual curiosities: What do you do? Are you married? What do you love? etc. While this is lovely and social, I invite them to speak only if they are speaking from their soul during the entire retreat. We were in silence for many hours of the day, which made this exercise easier, but during other times and especially speaking in the sharing circle we did every day, people were deeper and more sincere in their words. The listening too was amped up, as they really "heard" each other. Our mantra for the retreat was:

Is it kind?

Is it real?

Does it improve on the silence?

As a result, the writing and sharing is profound and the bonding that occurs in the groups is deep and rich.

Chapter Twenty-One

ILLUSION OF SEPARATION

The ocean cannot count
its drops of rain
So better to call it
One

The variety of facilitators booking Xenia over the years were always interesting, and I was often invited to many of the programs but attended very few. My absolute preference was silence as the teacher and teaching, but I did pass through many a great lesson in a variety of modalities before resting in the silence. There were two profound occasions I feel were meaningful to share with you:

1/ I was invited to a ceremony with a medicine man visiting from Peru. He carried a plant medicine reputed to have a profound, healing impact, in particular with addictions and various illnesses such as cancer. He offered it with utmost privacy and respect. I had received such an invite several times in the past but had declined, although I was curious. This time, though, when invited, I felt a clear *yes* arise from within. I didn't know what I was getting myself into but felt the truth of it, and so I began this journey on a Friday night with a group of people I hardly knew. There was little need for names, stories or big explanations; instead, a gentle acceptance of privacy and no need for small talk.

In the container of safety, love, and reverence, attendees sat in a circle, quietly watching the preparation of protocols for the ceremony. The ambience set with candles reflected shadows throughout the space, and the aroma of Aqua De Florida, (a healing, cleansing cologne) filled the senses. Anticipation flowed through my body. I was somewhat afraid but mostly excited. I could feel a kind of electric energy in the room.

The shaman explained a little about the medicine and the journey unfolding throughout the night and into the early morning hours. He mentioned it would prove useful to form an intention before drinking. Each person was invited, one at a time, to sit with him as he offered the special "brew" and listened to people as they whispered their intentions.

While I waited my turn, I told my body it was okay to welcome in this medicine. It would be safe, even though I felt unsure what could happen under its influence.

I didn't have a clear intention at first, but as I sat opposite the medicine man, I noticed the words stringing themselves together to pose the question: *How can I heal the illusion of separation?*

While I held onto this thought, I took the shot of medicine and swallowed it back quickly. It tasted ghastly, and I almost gagged but assured myself it was okay and I could handle it.

I went back to my little cosy spot with a sleeping bag, pillow, and a bucket (as suggested by the organizers) and pondered this question arising spontaneously from a deep place within. It was a concept I had mulled over for several years in my spiritual practice, but I couldn't say I really understood it. I knew, though, this particular configuration of words had the power to unlock a secret door. It offered a key, and I felt it go effortlessly into the lock and turn.

I sat patiently, watching in silence, the movement of people standing up and sitting with the medicine man to receive this potent elixir. One by one, a beautiful orchestration of trust and willingness occurred.

Soon, everyone got served, and beautiful chants from the plant spirits poured out through the medicine man as he beat his drum in exquisite rhythms. Reference to time and space disappeared as the body quivered with joy and delight. I saw colours and geometry extending beyond the normal seeing capacity. Sounds came crisp and vibrant, and I experienced a heightened sense of awareness.

Struck by the words sewn together to form the question, had I found the key to unlock the secrets of the universe? They were secrets stretching beyond the human mind and beyond all universes.

How can I heal the illusion of separation?

Soon, I was shown everything, and I will do my best to put into words what seems virtually impossible to explain.

First, I got shown *We Are All One*. I saw how we are indestructible, immortal energy substance (yet, ultimately, beyond substance) moving between formlessness and form, between un-manifest and manifest reality. Nothing or nobody is dying, only transforming. We are not separate at all. I got shown we are not these bodies but a dance of consciousness being played out for an experience.

I saw *I Am God* and so are you, and no difference exists between any of us except the form we have chosen, which in itself is an illusion. I saw how Mother Nature is also an appearance and not a fact.

It was as if we humans or "I/God" (which is more how I perceived it), said:

I know, let's play a game called being human. There will be some rules to this game called "a body having needs and conditions to unfold, and an ego mind generating the illusion of separation." There will be the job of having all the experiences possible for this thing called a human form. We will have the power to project various situations, circumstances, and people onto our screen of consciousness for the purpose of having an experience. Through this, hopefully, we will come to something called Compassion.

We will set up all these scenarios in our pathway in this game of life. And one special effect will provide the greatest elevation of all, and that is we will forget who we are and will have to begin the long, arduous journey of remembering. We will, therefore, live conditioned lives with specific scenarios to play out this game with the mistaken false belief we are separate mortal beings subject to something called death.

Wow, really! I was deeply moved.

Soon, I saw how emotions such as fear, terror, jealousy, pain, love, happiness, resentment, guilt, etc. get created. I recognised how circumstances played out, like murdering, getting murdered, becoming the victim, becoming the victimizer, and all the possibilities of being poor, rich, big, small, powerful, weak, etc. I saw the levels and hierarchy.

It seemed a game of polarities and limitation. Though, if you knew the game, you didn't have to get thrown around by it.

As I got shown one scenario after another, laughter overtook me, uncontrollable, deep, gut-wrenching laughter. I heard the thought, *"Ssssh ... stay quiet. Don't let them know you're awake. Don't let them know you know the game; otherwise, you won't be able to play anymore."* Oh no.

I saw and heard the pain of the people beside me in the ceremony; some groaned, others threw up. I saw their identification to their pain and bodies. I felt their attachment to the story the mind projected, and I felt a sudden laughter arise that was hard to suppress. I didn't want to laugh when so many seemed in pain, but it struck me as overwhelmingly funny when I got shown one image after another of the folly I had gotten involved in and the realization I had taken this thing called "my life" so seriously. I pushed my head into the pillow to thwart the waves of laughter.

Suddenly, Charlie—our potbellied pig—came onto the screen, and I remember thinking, *if everything is part of God, does this include Charlie?* at which point I could no longer contain the laughter. In my mind, I saw Charlie walking down the trail, so innocent, doing his job of being a pig. *Does he know he's a pig? Or does he know he's God also?* I could see no separation in him. He was pure love. He was in his role as a pig without any apology and without trying to get out of his part.

Becoming aware of the pain in the room and the diversity of experience, the thought came, *how can I see all this and still take life seriously? How can I have compassion for others still caught by the illusion and suffering?* It became so important to understand how to have compassion.

I went up to the medicine man with this enquiry, and it seemed all I could do not to laugh, because I could see his role. He was me, and I, he. I asked him, "How can I know the truth and still have compassion? I cannot stop laughing."

He said, "It is okay to laugh and see all this." Then he added, "As quietly as possible, though." Afterward, I went outside and saw a man standing by what appeared as a tree. I saw everything as appearance, moving into form and back to the formless state, and it felt so trippy to get invited behind the scenes, as it were, of this extraordinary game. I asked the man, "Who are you pretending to be?"

He said, "What? What did you say?"

I leaned forward so he could hear better and said, "I'm pretending to be Angelyn. Apparently, I own this place. Who are you pretending to be?"

All of a sudden, he broke out into laughter, obviously now in on the joke. We talked and laughed together for a while. It felt surreal, yet a knowing of truth overlay the experience beyond anything I had ever known before. Not wanting to intrude too much into his space, I made my way back to the yurt.

I wanted to pee first but had the thought that I should test the theory; if it is all an illusion, I can ignore my body's impulse to pee. I thought, well, if it's all an illusion, so is peeing. As it turned out, that theory wasn't fool proof. I darted into the bush to pee just in the nick of time. Interesting, I thought, and realised we still have to work with the needs of the physical body. Yes, that became one of the rules I got shown: the body has needs and a destiny to fulfil.

Throughout the night, I became aware of a growing compassion as I saw an image of people hiding under a blanket of mind oppression and suffering. I saw my role now was to live as this being called Angelyn. Would this be okay? Was it all right to live in this form, in this set of circumstances, at this apparent time? I got shown loving Self was all-important, and I felt immense gratitude arise.

Many quotes I had read previously filtered through my awareness, and I understood them at a far deeper level. I saw people who had held out the invitation to awaken and realised what they had said was true and they must have known all along; otherwise, they could not have spoken with such authority.

Byron Katie [12]says, *Forgiveness is realizing that what you thought happened, didn't.* I saw this as utterly true. If I project onto the screen an experience I want to have and it plays out, and I blame someone else for it, I do not understand the game. I, who set it up and, in fact, played it out, am responsible. I should not punish myself but free myself from this illusion so I can come home to rest and, mostly, to have compassion for *Self*.

The realization *I Am God and So Are You* became paramount. I had suspected this all along, but until this night and this direct experience, I could not know for certain.

Over the following days, everything filtered through this knowing. Now, I have an acceptance of my life as Angelyn and a surrendering to the great mystery. I have glimpsed the truth and feel satisfied with this life. Peace prevails from the deepest core of this being, most of the time (Not always . . . as the Zen masters say, "First, the enlightenment experience, and then you have to do the laundry").

---

[12] Byron Katie www.thework.com

2/   The second occasion was with a wonderful spiritual Advaita teacher, Pamela Wilson[13]. She had been doing a Satsang in Vancouver when I invited her to my retreat centre. Rather spontaneously, and to my great joy, she accepted.

Soon after we arrived, she offered to lead me in a heart meditation, and we decided the Sanctuary would be a wonderful place to do this. It was an interactive meditation, and I had never done one before and couldn't imagine how deep I could go while interacting.

Pamela oozes heart and love, and it was easy to fall into deep meditation with her in no time at all.

I won't share the full details here even though she did give me permission to use it, especially with teens and young adults. I will say it included letting go of old patterns, conditioning, time, roles, titles, pain, rules, ideas and finally everything.

Two hours later, in a flash of what appeared as thirty minutes, awareness took over and there was a total realization of my true nature.

While I had glimpses before and had read much about it, this was different. I thought it would include bliss and lights and love and all the good stuff. Instead, there was only darkness. Not scary darkness but simply

---

[13] Pamelawilson.com

darkness, or more like nothingness with a pulsation present and a full understanding that *I Am That*. I am this nothingness, this unmanifest potentiality. I did, in fact, exist; not as a person with a body but as this abiding nothingness of pure potentiality. This confirmed what I already had started to see and know.

From this direct experience I can no longer ever doubt or question this truth. There is no separation at the deepest core of existence.

That day with Pamela, I never wanted to leave the Sanctuary or talk again I was so peaceful but as life would have it, the body started moving and life carried on. But I will never forget this truth sits at the very foundation of my reality.

The Eternal Candle holds the space in the Sanctuary
for the Silent Retreats.

Chapter Twenty-Two

OUT OF THE SILENCE IT CAME

There are no fees at this level
Listen
Listen
Listen

 It is Xenia's twenty-fifth year and I couldn't be happier, more fulfilled or optimistic about the continuous journey of this magical sanctuary on the West Coast of Canada. A beautiful new young community has joined us, and we have never been more booked. Our passion for keeping the silence front and centre in our work is even more important as we proceed along on this journey.

In spite of all that is going on politically, environmentally, socially and globally, we are in an evolutionary time and we are waking up as a collective. We are waking up whether we think we are ready or not. More and more people are leaving the planet rather prematurely (according to the norm), and the younger ones, millennials, are being accused of being lazy and entitled. But I beg to differ. I would say they are stirring up the status quo, and why shouldn't they? It is time to do things differently, and I am happy to report it is happening at lightning speed even when it feels slow.

Much Happens when Nothing
Appears to be Happening

Globally, we are connected at levels never before attained, and though much of this is through technology, many are understanding the connectedness of us all through consciousness. "Stay in the heart, stay in the heart," as Wallace Black Elk told us way back eighteen years ago on 9/11.

As I wind down this book, I'd like to leave you, my reader and friend, with the most important lesson I have learned from being had by a vision and living in Radical Trust.

Ultimately at a deeper level, *it is all handled* and yes, you will need to do your spiritual practice and have courage, fortitude and resilience to go the distance with your dream. There were so many times I wanted to quit and walk away when it seemed too hard to bear, but once I surrendered into the fire and trusted implicitly my Dharmic life and guidance given, I never felt alone in my mission or plight. Not only did I have an awesome community of people working with me, it was clear the universe was abundantly supporting us. Money came, people came, and resources continued to flow towards this much-loved mission of Xenia. You know what I mean by this, because you have had these experiences, and if not, know this is available for you if you ask and are able to receive.

And if you choose to embark on your vision, you will be tested, you will wonder if you are going crazy and making things up. You will feel alone at times and despondent, but the more radical trust you have, the easier and more graceful the journey will be. Check out my book *Honour Your Calling*[14] for support regarding your life's mission and identifying what it is and how to honour this and live from a deep sense of purpose and fulfillment.

Out of the Silence It Came

What came? All of it. The messages, the inspiration, the vision, the directives and the road map, by using your left and right brain in equal stride as you honour your dream and vision. *Listen, listen, listen – there are no fees at this level.*

Notice this guidance is given to each one freely. But can you hear it? Do you feel and sense it? Can you receive it? Are you willing to take action upon it? Use nature and

---

[14] Honour Your Calling – The Professionals Guide to Quitting Your Job and Doing Your Soul Work. angelyntoth.com/books

silence to support you to listen deeply within. Watch for messages showing up in everyday life. Pay attention and keep moving forward as requested. Trust your heart to show you the way. Settle into what is right in front of you now. You will not be led astray; I can promise you.

Imagine wanting what you have and not wanting what you don't have. What could be easier? Our society is based on always striving and wanting more, and in the process, we have not received what we already have. Bringing our awareness to this and gratitude of what is, we start to come home.

Living as awareness in the movie of life, we feel happy and free, no longer attached to an outcome, but simply enjoying the ride. It may look like a passive approach, but I have found it to be a passionate and compelling way of living. I know with certainty that this life I walk in, appearing as a body, has a plan, a divine plan. I am not a mistake; I never was and never will be and all is happening in perfect order. It sounds easy, and it is, except mind loves security and this way of living is not secure according to the mind. The irony is that it is the only security. The Course in Miracles says: Nothing real can be threatened. Nothing unreal exists. Herein lies the peace of God.

Things don't happen to us; they happen for us; a subtle but profound difference.

Everything in life comes to awaken us to a deeper understanding of our true nature. If I do not receive what comes, then how am I living my life? Obviously, I'm caught in the past and in the future, thereby missing the very gift itself – the present. Letting feelings have their life as they arise naturally is to receive the gift they have come to deliver. Saying "yes" to what is, liberates us and from this place, natural intelligence and inspiration can shine through.

Everything we need we already have.

The question is, what do we have?

There is a treasure to be found in our present life circumstance. It is not always easy to find. As we awaken, we start to notice the beauty and perfection in everything. Our perception is the only thing causing any suffering. The stories we tell and the attitudes and concepts we hold dear keep us separate and give us a false sense of security. The mind keeps us busy wanting what we don't have and not wanting what we do have. That's its job.

As we inquire upon the thoughts we have taken to be truth and meet them with understanding, we move into stillness and begin finding grace in everything. From this place of acceptance, the capacity for deep peace increases.

Awareness awakens us to what is true and what is false. The body responds naturally as a yes and a no signal. If we override this response, we usually suffer the consequences. If we follow the natural movement of the body, we enter a place of surrender and freedom so eventually we are always responding as "yes." Yes to the no and yes to the yes. How can we trust this deep inner knowing to lead us in the direction of our deepest fulfillment? How can we get to know this yes/no response better?

How can we heal the illusion of separation? How can we find peace and rejoice in whatever life brings us?

Simply remember that whatever comes, comes to awaken, not to punish. Gratitude becomes the only true position to hold. We can trust that if it is brought into our life, it is in perfect order. This is true liberation.

Radical Trust

There is so much wisdom held within the flame

Into which the moth surrenders its life

Not from wisdom but from instinct

It has no choice

It cannot resist the attraction

Any more than you can

And the more you turn away

The more pain will surface

Be not afraid of such strong waves of pull

And with all the vigour of

The child leaping into water

Throw yourself in and know the Truth

You were thrown

—*Angelyn*

EPILOGUE

I just returned from India as the Pandemic of 2020 was taking hold. After a month of being in a completely different culture, stretching my entire existence with its extreme contrasts and contradictions, I am met with a continuation of acute change.

On the cusp of launching this book, I ask myself; is this book still relevant? Are the messages still consistent with my deepest knowing when our world is in a watershed moment?

Yes, of course it is. **Radical Trust** is more relevant now than ever before.

What has changed now is the connection I feel to the entire world as this situation is scaling up to include the whole planet. I see we are one world and therefore this pandemic is assigned for me, for you, for us, for the world. There are some who believe it is real and others who belief it is not. Whether it is or it isn't, the world has stopped on its axis in ways we have never experienced before globally. *What if there is a pathway beyond this polarity of right and wrong?*

If it's true that everything comes for us to use and evolve, it begs the question: What is this pandemic showing us?

For your hearts to repair the split it received when you became so busy and reckless with your energy and grace. For your loss of connection with your brothers and sisters of all communities around the entire world. The loyalty and downright obsession you have awarded the technology in your hands. Why is this? Advancement, evolution...? Perhaps. Or was it the fear that wedged the gap of separation between your head, heart, soul and spirit. The separation started within and manifests without. All are on what appears as a separate journey, but none truly walk alone for when you take your consciousness to the highest possible level, you will know the connectedness with all of reality. All is one and one cannot exist apart from the other.

As you come into your heart and presence there is no separation, even though life is individual. There is an awakening happening across the entire world because it is time and it has been planned.

It was forecast not as some epic destruction of humanity but as the dissolution of the ego. The world ego is collapsing, and the world heart has the opportunity to lead all out of the darkness into the light of day if one is ready. If you are not ready what are you resisting and saying "no" to? This is important, it is very important.

As you say yes and walk forward upon this present reality, everything will be shown to you in each moment arising. *Worry and fear create a wall to the truth and to the heart knowing itself in full and complete union with the divine. Stay out of these divergent energies the moment you feel them arising.*

How?

By watching them fully and completely with a heart of compassion and they will yield to the light. Be comfortable in not knowing everything ahead of taking your steps. Be willing to step into the unknown like never before has happened for you. Not once or twice but always, as a way of life. In total and complete surrender to the intrinsic nature of your soul. So that your individuated soul can merge with the one soul and complete its journey to enlightenment. Yes, mass enlightenment for your planet is the possibility at this time. Fear not anything of the physical world for all will be provided as needed. Let go and let God like never before. And so it is.

ACKNOWLEDGMENTS

Kasara Toth, Chrystalle Grace, Saria Suzan Bailey, Elinor Meney, Ellen Hayakawa, Diane Leclair, Alexander Brumm, Ariel & Shea Cantin, Jessie Flynn, Bernard Leclair, Matthew Smith & Deborah Bramm, Dale Hamilton & Sheena Ashdown, Tarla Curran, Arlette Alexander, Brian Silver, Mike Mommersteeg, Jamie Arnold, Wendy Sobieski, Marina Richards, Junie Swadron, Julie Blue, Sage Barrett, Carol and Frank Kemble, John and Patricia Hogarth, Gary Wilcox, Morganne Keplar, Andy and Mary Hoppenrath, Robert Keagan, Doug Stelling, Renee Beth Poindexter, Tah Kwan, Al & Jan Keranen, Harry Mathers, Sara Spicer, Dr. Neil Tessler, Aimee Burton, Chad Babcock, Matt Learning, Maggie Calder, Stephen Cherniske, Bill Lee, Dr. Ralph Bietz, and my Univera Team, you know who you are.

ABOUT THE AUTHOR

Angelyn Toth is a mother, grandmother, partner, author, CEO of Leading-Edge Creative Development and owner/founder of **Xenia** Retreat Centre on Bowen Island, BC. Canada. Xenia was founded in 1994, attracting people from all  over the world into its loving, and delightful sanctuary. Her mission is, *to support people to move beyond resistance to their highest and best self and trust their soul essence to guide them.* In collaboration with a faculty of conscious entrepreneurs whose commitment is to serve people waking up and sharing their greatest gifts in service to humanity, she has developed a global program, OPA – Opening Pathways of Awareness.

Angelyn has been a top leader in Univera since 2005 and values greatly the transformational quality offered in this work. Winning most of the company's awards for exemplary leadership she was inducted into the Millionaire Club having personally earned over one million dollars in her first few years. She won the highest award for leadership, integrity and service, the *Yun Ho Lee* Award. https://www.youtube.com/watch?v=Rh_LtPBck00

Her passion for animals and transformation was combined in her book **From Squeak to Roar,** *Unleashing the Potential in your Relationship Marketing Tribe.* She also wrote **Honour Your Calling,** The Professional's Guide to Quitting Your Job and Doing Your Soul Work, and now Angelyn gives you this book, **Radical Trust** *Manifesting a Vision When It Seems Impossible.*

In January 2020 she and her partner spent a month in India to deepen their spiritual path with yoga and meditation.

MYSTICAL TREASURES

The little verses at the beginning of each chapter are part of the Mystical Treasures book Angelyn wrote or rather, wrote her. For two weeks at 3:00 a.m. every morning she was summoned out of a deep sleep and asked to write down the words. There were over 250 of these little odes, similar to a modern haiku and you will find them on my website. The words were scribbled down on a notepad beside her bed and in the morning, she would decipher the words and their meaning.

THANK YOU

Thank you for reading my book. I hope you enjoyed my story and got some inspiration for your dream vision.

Subscribe to my mailing list and get posts and updates straight to your inbox! angelyntoth.com.

Sign-up now and get FREE access to my recording of The Story of Cabroi, a unique tale of transformation and discovery for children and adults alike. Through the use of metaphor, I will show you exquisite ways to achieve your highest potential.

Check out my web site angelyntoth.com or the retreat xeniacentre.com to find out more about our 90-Day OPA Global Program and other inspiring programs like our 9 Day Silent Retreats and Writer's Retreats.

WAYS OF CONTACTING ANGELYN

Website: angelyntoth.com
Email: angelyn@angelyntoth.com
Xenia Retreat Centre: xeniacentre.com
Call: 604-947-9816

Published by: xeniacreations.com

Made in the USA
Columbia, SC
10 August 2020

14413378R00152